# Calling Upon Angels

## How Angels Help Us in Daily Life

# Calling Upon Angels

How Angels Help Us in Daily Life

Rosemary Ellen Guiley

Visionary Living, Inc.
New Milford, Connecticut

*Calling Upon Angels: How Angels Help Us in Daily Life*

By Rosemary Ellen Guiley

Cover design: Robert Michael Place,
from The Burning Serpent Oracle deck. Used with permission.
Back jacket and interior design by Leslie McAllister

ISBN: 978-0-9860778-6-9 (pbk.)
ISBN: 978-0-9860778-7-6 (e-pub)

Published by Visionary Living, Inc.
New Milford, Connecticut
www.visionaryliving.com

## Other books by Rosemary Ellen Guiley available from Visionary Living

*Dreamwork for Visionary Living*
*Dream Messages from the Afterlife*
*Pocket Dream Guide and Dictionary*
*Develop Your Miracle Mind Consciousness*
*Angel Magic for Love and Relationships*
*Christmas Angels: True Stories of Hope and Healing*
*Soul Journeys: Past and Future Lives*
*Haunted by the Things You Love*
*The Djinn Connection*
*The Art of Black Mirror Scrying*
*Guide to the Dark Side of the Paranormal*

# Table of Contents

# Introduction

Angels have been part of my life since childhood. When I was young, I experienced them as comforting beings who were close around me, especially at night when I went to sleep, and often when I was alone and occupying myself at play. They sang, and they had beautiful voices.

I thought everyone felt and heard angels. When I got older and discovered that my experiences were not shared by all, even though they were not unique to me, I was curious to know why. Why do people not have the same awareness of beings and phenomena that exist on the fringes of physical reality? My experience of, and interest in angels, were among the many otherworldly facets of my life that led to the work that I do now in metaphysics and the paranormal.

Angels are extraordinary beings, full of majesty and power. They have played important roles in the development of human beings, and they are still at work today. Whether we actively believe in them or not, we are likely to cross paths with them at various points in the life journey. If we make an intention to connect with them, a cosmic vista—the window to eternity—opens.

This book is an introduction to the angel realm, with perspectives from Biblical times to modern, and how people today experience and interact with angels. Angels are timeless; only the trappings of our experiences of them change.

In my research, I interviewed people on both sides of the Atlantic, from everyday individuals to healers to mediums and channelers and more. There is a great deal of wisdom in all of the points of view. I devoted entire chapters to Eddie Burks, an extraordinary medium in England (now passed), and Ken Cohen, an exceptional healer in Native American and Qigong traditions, both of whom shared profound insights not only into angels, but also into the relationship between human beings and the Creator. Angels minister over all things in creation, and one of their primary functions concerning humans is to connect humanity to God.

I have included some of my own experiences as well as the experiences of others (some from my earlier work *Angels of Mercy*), which demonstrate the many ways we are benefited and influenced by angels. I discuss the forms and characteristics of angels; the nature of guardian angels; the ways angels intervene in earthly affairs; and how we can recognize their presence. Angels are not always obvious, and often manifest in subtle ways. Even when subtle, they have a big impact.

Angels are in a renaissance of interest. More and more people want to know who they are, what they are doing, and how we can connect with them to improve our lives and make the world a better place. The answers to those questions are explored in this book.

# 1

# Enter Angels

Robert S., an industrial electrician from Trenton, New Jersey, owes his life to an angel. While working in a mill, he grabbed hold of a killer 440-volt wire that he didn't know was live. As he felt the electricity surge through his body, he thought, "My God, I don't want to die!"

Instantly, he was pulled off the wire by an invisible pair of hands around his waist. He was hurled violently backwards and fell to the floor. The next thing he knew, he was lying on his back, looking up at a coworker. He should have been dead.

Robert's coworkers said that his life had been saved by the fact that he was wearing new shoes that day, and the thick rubber soles afforded insulation. Robert believes differently. "I felt something pull me off," he said. "Something saved my life. I thank God I'm alive."

That "something," he is convinced, was his guardian angel.

Robert suffered third-degree burns and lost a little finger to gangrene. Within two years of the accident, he developed psoriasis. Irritated patches of skin appeared around his waist. One day, he noticed that the patches lined up with the imprint of hands. The association was eerie, and reinforced his conviction that divine intervention on the part of one of God's messengers had rescued him from death. The experience had a profound impact on him. Like most people who have an extraordinary experience involving the unknown, he had difficulty talking about it to others. When he related the story to me, he hadn't mentioned it to anyone for years.

For Aimee L. of Cambria, California, her angelic rescuer appeared in the form of a human being. Here is her account:

> I was in a hospital suffering from some rare throat virus that caused me to cough so violently, I would begin to strangle. During one of those fits in the middle of the night, I called for a nurse. No one came right away, and I began to panic, for I couldn't breathe.
>
> Suddenly the door flew open and a short, stocky nurse came bursting in, and with a voice of authority said, "Close your mouth and breathe through your nose."
>
> When I gestured that no air would come through my nose, she clamped her hand over my mouth and shouted, "Breathe!"
>
> And, breathe I did and I stopped choking.
>
> Her next words were, "Just can't understand why they haven't taught you that." And out she went.
>
> Because I wanted to thank her, the next morning I asked the nurse who was it who was on night duty. When she asked me to describe her, she looked puzzled and said that description didn't fit anyone on their staff, but she would check on it.
>
> Later, the head nurse came in and asked me to describe the nurse again. She said there was no one employed there who came close to my description. When I asked why they hadn't instructed me on what to do when I began to strangle, they said they had never heard of the method.
>
> The doctor's response to the experience was interesting. He knew about the method, but why he hadn't

told me, I'll never know. But he whispered in my ear, "I think you met an angel." By then, I was convinced I had.

There have been a few times in my life when an almost overpowering aroma of flowers would occur, when no flowers were near. With it was always a sensation of euphoria. I do not think that I am anyone "special" because of these experiences. But, through them and other spiritual happenings, I know we are here to evolve back to the spirit that we truly are. And once we believe we are not victims of life, but the creators of our reality, all manner of beautiful manifestations appear in our life.

Robert and Aimee have plenty of company. For the past several decades, angels have made a tremendous comeback, and have undergone a resurgence of popularity. More than at any other time in modern history, people are believing in angels, are talking about their encounters with them, and learning how to communicate with them.

## From the ashes of obscurity

Not long ago, angels gathered dust, consigned to art and Christmas cards. Many people scoffed at the idea that angels might be real. Even in the early 1980s, Dutch physician H.C. Moolenburgh found that people laughed at him when he asked if they believed in angels, or had ever encountered an angel. A few people who admitted having encounters with angels were afraid to talk about them, out of fear that others would think they were crazy. Undaunted, Moolenburgh wrote *A Handbook of Angels*, which struck a secret chord and became an international hit.

Similarly, French journalist Georges Huber encountered a great deal of skepticism about angels when he began research for his book, *My Angel Will Go Before You*, published in 1983. Huber virtually apologizes for his interest in angels, in an age where science and technology make them seem hopelessly out of date and the stuff of fairy tales. A later preface to his book from Sighard Kleiner, Abbot General of the Cistercians, comments, "I was very surprised to learn recently that you were going to bring out a book on angels. A journalist, even though he is well versed in theology: isn't that a rather daring subject for him to choose? Don't journalists always go where the wind blows? You could scarcely say the wind is blowing around angels these days."

The ecclesiastical world was for many years almost embarrassed over the question of the existence of angels. Various church figures from various denominations said angels were "out of touch with reality" and thus endangered our belief in the Gospels, adding that it would be best for all if angels disappeared from the liturgy, sermons, and public awareness.

Writing in 1969, Cardinal G.M. Garrone, the Archbishop of Toulouse, stated, "It is an understatement to say that angels have gone out of style. We prefer not to think of them for fear of being confronted with a painful and insoluble dilemma. Either we must affirm with the Church the existence of these mysterious beings and thus find ourselves in the disagreeable company of the naive and uninformed, or else frankly speak out against their existence and be in the equally unpleasant situation of rejecting the faith of the Church and the obvious meaning of the Gospels. The majority, therefore, choose to express no opinion at all."

Angels, however, refuse to be consigned to a liturgical waste bin. Popular belief in them may have gone underground, but never went away. Belief in angels is now at an all-time high, rivaling the level of angel beliefs that peaked during the Middle Ages. More than ever, we *need* angels.

## New popularity

There are many reasons for the return of angels. Perhaps the leading factor is a collective sense of lack of control. Every day, we turn on the radio or television and get a barrage of bad news. We feel overwhelmed by pressures and circumstances that seem beyond our influence: drugs, crime, homelessness, economic problems, political and social instability, war, disease, famine, and an increasingly toxic environment. We long for help, including a divine intervention that, if it cannot change things on a large scale, at least can brighten our own personal sphere.

Another significant factor in the popularity of angels is that they are an appealing form of divine intervention. Unlike the Judeo-Christian God, who is abstract and has no form or face, angels are personable. According to our mythology, they can assume the form of beautiful humans. They are loving, benevolent, wise, patient and capable of bestowing miracles—so we perceive them to be (according to Scripture, however, angels will punish humans if that is God's directive.) We view angels as always with us—they never desert us, no matter how poorly we perform. And even though they do not always save us from catastrophe, they stand ready as a source of strength to help us through all our trials. We seem to have a great, collective hunger for spiritual guidance that is personal and intimate, a hunger that is not being met through conventional religion. Angels are our personal companions, our guides, our protectors.

Another major factor in their current popularity is our increasing openness to paranormal experience. Popular interest in the paranormal and things spiritual has gone through cycles in the past. The present interest is part of the so-called Aquarian Age or New Age, which gained momentum around the 1960s. In the 1980s, actress Shirley MacLaine encouraged candor and exploration with publication of her own spiritual quests.

## Michael's request

A most unusual angel encounter, which involved the archangel Michael, happened to a dear friend of mine, Juliet Hollister, of Greenwich, Connecticut. The encounter is unusual because it featured a vivid visual apparition, clear telepathic communication, some odd synchronicities with other people—and a demonstration that even angels like to have a good time.

Juliet founded the Temple of Understanding, the second oldest interfaith organization in the world. Its purpose is to be a "spiritual United Nations, promoting understanding between and about the world's religions. Juliet conceived of the idea for the Temple in 1959, and launched it with the help of Eleanor Roosevelt. To build the Temple, Juliet traveled the world and has had audiences with, and has been entertained by, an impressive list of heads of state, spiritual leaders and other luminaries. She met three popes—Paul II, John XXIII, and John Paul—as well as the Dalai Lama, with whom she corresponded regularly. She traveled to some of the remotest and wildest corners of the earth.

Before she passed away a few years ago, Juliet packed more adventures and accomplishments into the second half of her life than most people could manage in several lifetimes. Friends called her a "spiritual Auntie Mame," a moniker that suited her well—she was charming, sophisticated, funny, and irreverent, and always ready to set off on yet another adventure.

One might think that Juliet's work with the leaders of the world's major religions would have brought her into constant contact with the angel kingdom. Far from it. Many of those leaders with whom she worked were openly skeptical of the existence of angels and considered them to be only metaphors or literary devices. Consequently, for the first twenty-five years that Juliet was developing the Temple of Understanding, she kept quiet about her own beliefs and experiences.

Her earliest encounter with the spirit realms took place when she was a child growing up in a suburb of New York. Her mother was a Christian Scientist and former Baltimore debutante. Juliet was fond of her maternal grandfather, and looked forward every summer to visits at his home, Bunker Hill Farms, outside of Baltimore.

One afternoon in 1920, when Juliet was eight, her mother told her, "Grandpa has gone to another world." Two years later, when Juliet once again visited Bunker Hill Farms, she looked up from playing in the garden to see Grandpa, looking solid and real as if he were still alive. She received a mental message: "Surprised, aren't you, little granddaughter. I just popped by to let you know I am keeping an eye on you." Then he was gone.

Juliet told her mother, who dismissed the episode as a trick of afternoon sunlight and a child's imagination. Juliet knew better, and repressed talking about Grandpa's visit. It marked her first spiritual turning point, for it sparked a curiosity to investigate other religions.

"I have always believed in angels," Juliet told me one snowy winter morning as we sat in her cozy Greenwich cottage furnished with items collected on her round-the-world adventures. Like her experience with her grandfather, she kept these beliefs private, lest others disapprove.

One of her first angel events was a vicarious experience through her young son, Dickerman. Dickie, as Juliet called him when he was small, became interested in angels when he was about five or six years old—the most common age for an initial "extraordinary experience."

One day Dickie announced to Juliet, "More than anything in the world, I want to see an angel. Can you do something to help, Mom?"

Juliet thought for a moment. "Every night after I tuck you into bed and you say your prayers, why don't you quietly ask an angel to come and see you?" She wasn't at all sure that this request would work, but she felt I had to say something.

Dickie thought it was a good idea. So, every night he asked for an angel to come. But nothing happened. About once a week he would say to Juliet, "No angel, but I'm keeping asking, Mom." He seemed so earnest and patient.

After a while, Juliet got a little cross with the angelic kingdom for not responding. Finally one day Dickie burst into his parents' bedroom at six in the morning, bounced on the bed, and announced, "The angel came, Mom!" He was *so* excited.

Juliet was thrilled. "Tell me all about it," she urged.

"He was huge, standing in the corner of my bedroom," said Dickie. "I felt all this wonderful warm loving thing, and I knew it was an angel."

"What did he look like? Was it a boy or a girl?"

"I really don't know," answered Dickie, "because the angel told me that he was afraid that if I looked into his face, it would be so full of light that I would be frightened. So he purposely kept his back to me."

That was Dickie's only visit by an angel—at least that he ever talked about.

Juliet's encounter with the archangel Michael took place in October 1984, as she was preparing for the sixth Spirit Summit Conference sponsored by the Temple of Understanding. The first conference had been held in India in 1968, and others had followed at intervals of several years in Geneva and in the United States. This sixth conference was to take place at St. John the Divine, the largest Gothic cathedral in the world, located on the Upper West Side in Manhattan. Numerous luminaries of the ecclesiastical and political worlds were featured guests, including His Holiness the Dalai Lama of Tibet, Tenzin Gyatso, and Dr. Robert Mueller, then assistant secretary-general of the United Nations. The audience was expected to number eight to ten thousand people—a standing room only crowd inside the giant and elegant cathedral.

At the end of the day-long conference, a candlelight ceremony was scheduled to take place. Religious leaders would carry candles to the center altar and offer prayers from their respective religions. Juliet was to be included in this ceremony, delivering a fifteen-minute talk on the Temple, its purpose and its activities.

The prospect of making a speech in front of so many of the world's religious leaders and such a huge audience made Juliet nervous. She slaved away over her speech, and rehearsed it again and again.

The conference was on Saturday in October. The final rehearsal was slated for the Friday night before. Juliet traveled from her Connecticut home to Manhattan on Friday afternoon and settled into a room at the Cosmopolitan Club, located at 66th Street and Park Avenue on the East Side. She took a shower and lay down to rest.

As she was about ready to rise and dress, Juliet suddenly became aware of a presence in the form of a huge column of light standing at the foot of her bed. She perceived the outline of a figure and sensed that it was an angel, though she did not see wings or a face.

Juliet was startled but not frightened. She had believed in angels all of her life, and knew they didn't show up without good reason—just to check out a hairdo, as she put it later. As she studied it, the presence began to communicate telepathically with her.

"You're going to be speaking at the cathedral, and angels have a lot to do with holy, sacred places," the angel told her. "We guard them. Millions of people don't believe in us, but we are real entities. On behalf of the angelic kingdom, we would appreciate it if, when you make your speech, you would tell the people about us, that we are real, that we love the human race, and that we would like to work on behalf of it. But we can't unless we're invited to do so. We don't enter the life of a human unless we are asked. We are very eager to help."

This message overwhelmed Juliet. Never had she thought of saying anything about angels in her little speech. She replied to the figure of light, "I really do believe you're an angel. In fact, I kind of think you're the archangel Michael, although there's no reason why I should have one of the top ones show up. I'd love to do anything to help this planet and all the people on it, but I don't altogether trust myself here. I tell you what, I'll make a bargain with you. I'll do it if you do something to confirm that I'm not hallucinating, that I've got this straight."

The form of light disappeared without a response.

Juliet rose, dressed and walked down to the corner of 66th Street and Park Avenue to hail a taxi to go to the cathedral. It was a blowing, cold Friday evening at rush hour. Anyone who has ever been in New York City under those conditions knows how difficult it is to find a free taxi. Dozens and dozens roar by, all occupied, no matter where you are in that huge city. Juliet stood on the corner waiting in vain for a cab. Fifteen, twenty minutes went by. She grew anxious about arriving on time for the rehearsal.

Then she was struck by what seemed to be a brilliant idea. In retrospect, she believed the idea was planted by the angelic form that had visited her in the room. "They can do that, give us ideas," she told me.

Juliet said out loud, "Okay, Michael, here's your chance. I'm in a jam. I've got to get up to the cathedral and I'm running late. Surely in all of Manhattan, you can find *one* cab that's empty!"

Within minutes, a free cab pulled up and she hopped in. But the proof of the visiting angel's reality did not end there.

Juliet grew up in New York City and had been in hundreds of cabs. She always looked at the dashboard for the driver's photos of his children or wife, or little images of saints, Jesus, or the Virgin Mary that are commonly fastened to the dash. But in all her years, she had never seen anything like what greeted her that evening. There stuck onto the dashboard was a cheap plastic statue of a winged figure that bore the words, "The Right Archangel Michael." It was huge—about a foot high.

For a moment, Juliet could not speak. This was too weird—even synchronicity seemed unable to explain this incredible "coincidence."

The driver was named Tony, according to the license visible on the dash. Finding her voice, Juliet stammered, "Tony, tell me, what are you doing with the archangel Michael here in your cab?"

Tony turned to her and said, "Lady, let me tell you, he's a special friend of mine—he's my best friend Mike!"

"Your friend *Mike*?"

"You don't know about Mike?" Tony asked. "Hey, he's the greatest! Let me tell you, my wife, she gets mad at me, she throws the spaghetti across the kitchen or whatever, I call on Mike and ask him, how do you handle women. The kids get in trouble in school, I call on Mike. I can't pay the rent, I call on Mike. I really recommend him to you—he can do anything! Of *course* I have him in my cab. Who else would I have?"

All the way from 66th and Park to 110th Street and Amsterdam Avenue, Juliet heard a lecture on the virtues of the archangel Michael, and why he was Tony's best and greatest friend. At St. John the Divine, she got out and paid Tony, and he drove off, his statue of Michael standing like a guiding beacon on the dash.

Juliet said to herself, "All right, Juliet, you asked for a message, and now you've got to keep your promise." She was determined to keep up her end of the deal, despite some trepidation at the response of ecclesiastical authorities to a message that angels are real.

The following night at the conclusion of the conference—a huge success—Juliet gave her little speech, and talked about how angels are not just pretty Renaissance paintings. They are real, she informed the thousands in attendance, and they desire to help humanity, but they cannot do so unless humans ask for their help.

To Juliet's relief, no one recoiled in disbelief. In fact, for weeks afterward, she received an avalanche of mail, more than she had ever received in her life. The letters were testimony about people's own beliefs and experiences with angels. "They *are* real!" was the overall enthusiastic response.

I asked Juliet how that experience changed her own beliefs about angels.

"I didn't know they had such a sense of humor," she replied. "I felt the archangel himself was getting such a kick out of what was going on in that cab."

Juliet was also struck by the sense of sadness or loneliness about the figure of light that appeared in her room. "It seemed that the angels are hungry for communion with the human condition," she said. "Think of all the things a lifetime can bring—tragedy, heartbreak—and they would like to bring us hope. But it's like they're saying, 'Nobody's asked us to the party.'"

For the rest of her life, Juliet called on angels for help "day and night," as she described it. "I feel very close to them, I talk to them," she said. "If I didn't believe in the angel kingdom, I'd never be doing what I'm doing now—there would be no Temple of Understanding. I'm not alone in this—there's something far wiser helping me out. I have friends, pals." She added somewhat wistfully, "But I haven't had any experience quite like that since."

**To test our character**
Sometimes God sends angels among us disguised as humans to test us. The Bible says in Genesis 18 that when Abraham was camped on the plains of Mamre, three men appeared before his tent. He welcomed the strangers, and refreshed them with food and drink. Abraham was informed that Sarah, his wife, would bear a son. The idea seemed preposterous, for both Abraham and Sarah were quite old, and Sarah had never had children. Soon, she bore a son, Isaac.

Years ago, Ruth Beck, of North Hollywood, California, was visited by a mysterious stranger one day as she was about to leave her house. She shared with me the following account:

My three children, ages ten, eight and seven years, were waiting for me in the car. I had to close the doors and turn the lights off. Just as I turned the kitchen light off, I heard a knock on the front door. Thinking it was one of the children in the car playing a prank on me, I opened the door. Standing in front of me, to my surprise, was a very tall, handsome stranger. He was very clean, clothes were pressed, all in black. I took special notice that he wore a cloak with a shoulder-length cape effect.

He smiled and said, "Could you give me something to eat? I've been on the road two days and have a long way yet to go."

Startled, I thought, "I'm in a hurry." Then I pondered, "What shall I give him?" There were just two eggs in the box. I hurriedly scrambled them, and buttered two slices of bread, and made a nice sandwich. I put wax paper around it and put it in a paper bag. I added hot coffee to a bit of milk in the milk carton, then put it in a thick white mug, and took it all out to him. He smiled and thanked me.

"Then I turned the lights out and went to join the children in the car. They said, "What took you so long?"

I replied, "Why, didn't you see, I fed that man on the porch."

They said, "What man?"

He would have had to pass the car twice to get on the porch. I said, "Let's go look." They hopped out of the car, and we all stood a few paces from the car. It wasn't dark yet. There were no trees, houses, or anything to obstruct our view. We could see no one!

I believe God sent this to me as a test to see if I were too much in a hurry to stop and assist someone in need. I also believe that someday, as a token of remembrance, the cup will be returned to me."

These are but a few of the ways that angels enter our world. No two experiences are ever the same, yet they share similar circumstances and characteristics.

What are the factors that have shaped our beliefs about angels?

# 2

# Between Heaven and Earth

Angels are spiritual beings who inhabit a plane of existence between the human and the divine, transmitting messages and acting out divine will. This is an ancient concept familiar to many religions and cultures. Today's concepts of angels evolved from a long and rich heritage of Zoroastrian, Babylonian, Persian, Egyptian, Sumerian, Hebrew, and Greek faiths.

The word *angel* itself is derived from the Greek *angelos*, a translation of the Persian word *angaros*, or "courier." The Hebrew term is *mal'akh*, meaning "messenger" or "envoy," and is used in five different senses in Scripture:

1. The Word, given by God to the world
2. St. John the Baptist, the precursor of the messiah
3. Priests, who act as God's ambassadors to people
4. Prophets
5. Angels

Most often the term "messenger" or "envoy" is used in Scripture to mean angels. Messenger is only one of their functions, and these enlightened spirits can be found worldwide in many spiritual traditions, playing many roles.

## History of the angel

Intermediary beings are part of all mythologies. Precursors of angels that were supernatural winged creatures have been found in ancient Mesopotamia and Sumer. The Assyrian *karibu* (the source of the word *cherubim*), were fierce, winged beasts possessing features both animal and human. The role of the angel as protector can perhaps be traced to these ancestors, which acted as temple guardians.

The Greeks made a significant contribution to angel lore with their gods, such as Hermes, the winged messenger. Hermes is often credited as being the inspiration for archangel Michael, for many of the Greek gods were molded into angels by the Church in its attempt to convert the pagans. The Greeks also believed in *daimones*, spirits who came in both good and evil forms. The good ones were protectors, and the bad ones tried to lure people astray. People had one of each, who created a constant push and pull between good and bad. Socrates spoke of his *daimones*, who whispered in his ear. *Daimones* were absorbed into demons in Christianity, but in the process became solely evil.

The Aryans, who arrived in India and Persia around 2500 BC, believed in *devas* "shining ones"), who were deities subordinate to their supreme god, Dyeus. Perhaps it was from them that angels inherited their most salient characteristic—the ability to shine, or radiate light. The "el" suffix so common in angel" names is understood in several languages to mean "shining" or "radiant."

Devas made their way into the *Veda*, a collection of early sacred Hindu writings, where they were depicted in a hierarchical (but still polytheistic) arrangement. According the *Veda*, devas existed in the three worlds—Earth, Heaven and a spiritual realm in between. They were closely aligned with the elements of nature—fire, water, earth and air—which were considered expressions of their existence. Devas of water, for example, were assigned the feminine role of caretakers and nourishers of all living things.

Devas also found their way into Zoroastrianism, the religion founded by the prophet Zoroaster (Zarathustra) in Persia in the sixth century BC. It was through Zoroastrianism that devas evolved into angels. In founding this monotheistic faith, Zoroaster rejected the pantheism of the Hindus and offered instead a single, supreme deity, Ahura Mazda, locked in an eternal struggle against his evil enemy Ahaitin. Mazda is aided in this struggle by the good deeds of humans. He is also aided by seven archangels, the *amesha spentas*, who are the gods of Babylon and Assyria recycled into roles more appropriate to a monotheistic religion. They represent the concepts of wisdom, truth, immortality, deserved good luck, piety, salvation, and obedience. Each angel also acts as the guardian of something—fire, for example. *Yazatas* are another kind of Zoroastrian angels, and, like devas before them, they rule the elements.

Zoroastrian concepts of angelic beings were absorbed into Judaism, Christianity, and Islam. Islam's *malaika* ("messengers") are androgynous beings made of light who act as guardians of humans. Their names and personalities are borrowed from Judeo-Christian angels—for example, Mika'il (Michael) and Djibril (Gabriel).

## Judeo-Christian angels

Zoroastrianism was popular during the Hebrews' captivity in Persia and made its mark on their biblical writings. While their religion did not allow for any gods other than Yahweh, the idea of angelic intermediaries to the Divinity was acceptable and adoptable.

Angels are keepers of the cosmic order and guides to heaven in the early Merkabah mystical tradition, where some of them, hostile to humans, acted as barriers to the ascent to God. The Kabbalah, a collection of secret writings containing mystical knowledge that is passed on orally to those advanced enough to comprehend it, developed in the Middle Ages. Angels have associations with the *sephirot*, vessels for the emanations of God, known as Grace, Wisdom, Splendor, Understanding, Knowledge, Foundation, Eternity, Power, Beauty, and Crown. They stand together to form a tree—the Tree of Life.

At the top of the tree is the Angel of the Lord, Metatron, who gave the wisdom of the Kabbalah to humanity. He is considered in some accounts to be the greatest of the angels—there is scarcely an angelic duty or function that is not related to him. Metatron also figures in the Merkabah mysticism.

The etymology of "Metatron" is unclear. Possibly, the name itself was intended to be a secret, and may have been produced through a glossolalia-type of altered state of consciousness. Glossolalia is speaking in tongues, and is perhaps best-known for its part in charismatic religions. Metatron is sometimes called "the Prince of the Countenance," meaning he is the chief angel of those angels who are privileged to look upon the countenance of God.

Descriptions of him tell of a spirit or pillar of fire with 36 pairs of wings and myriad eyes. His face is more dazzling than the sun. He serves as God's Angel of Death, instructing the archangels Gabriel and Samael which human souls to take at any given moment.

### Enoch's seven heavens

Most of what we know about angels—their names, duties, and activities—comes from texts outside the Bible. The Bible offers few specifics about angels, and names only two: Michael ("who is as God"), and Gabriel ("God is my strength"). The catholic canon includes the book of Tobit, which features Raphael. According to Revelation in the New Testament, there are seven archangels who stand before God, but we are left to guess at the identities of the others.

Most of the angel lore that has been handed down through the centuries comes from the apocrypha ("hidden books"), writings that were declared heretical by the Church for one reason or another, such as lack of historical authenticity, and divergences from the core dogma of the developing church.

One of the apocryphal texts that gives the most information about angels is the book of Enoch, which has survived in three versions.

Enoch was a prophet who was so spiritually advanced that God had angels take him directly to heaven to record what he saw. His experiences enlightened him so much that God turned him into the angel Metatron.

The Enoch manuscripts were probably written by a number of anonymous authors between the second century BC and sixth century AD, although some scholars place them much later. The Enoch writings were declared apocryphal in the fourth century by St. Jerome. One of the chief objections to them was that they portrayed a multi-layered heaven that contains hell, populated by fallen angels. The concept of hell within heaven contradicted the dogma of the early church.

Enoch's accounts of visiting heaven and communing with angels are compelling reading. His heavenly adventures began one day when he was 365 years old, and was asleep on his couch. A "great distress" came into his heart, which he could not understand. Two beings appeared before him, which he described as men.

> And there appeared to me two men, exceedingly big, so that I never saw such on earth; their faces were shining like the sun, their eyes too *were* like a burning light, and from their lips was fire coming forth with clothing and singing of various kinds in appearance purple, their wings *were* brighter than gold, their hands whiter than snow.

Enoch was frightened, but the angels assured him to fear not—they had been sent by God to take him into heaven. They bore him up on their wings to the clouds to the first heaven. Enoch found seven heavens and seven corresponding earths, all united to each other by hooks. Beyond the seventh heaven were three more heavens.

The first heaven, ruled by Gabriel, was the one closest to Earth, and contained the winds and the clouds. The angels who lived here were astronomers and ruled the stars and heavenly bodies. There also were angels who were guardians of ice, snow, flowers and dew.

The second heaven was ruled by Raphael and was a dark penal area where fallen angels awaited judgment. His guiding angels, said Enoch:

> ...showed me darkness, and there I saw prisoners hanging, watched, awaiting the great and boundless judgment, and these angels were dark-looking, more than earthly darkness, and incessantly making weeping through all hours.

Enoch was told that these prisoners were "God's apostates," fallen angels who had turned away from God with their prince, who was fastened in the fifth heaven.

The fallen angels asked Enoch to pray for them. He wondered how he, a mere mortal man, could pray for angels. And if he did so, then who would pray for him? (This idea of angels begging for the mercy of a mortal probably contributed to the expulsion of the book of Enoch from canonical literature.)

The third heaven was ruled by Anahel and was a land of contrasts. One part of this heaven, the northern section, was actually hell, ice cold and sulfurous, filled with torturing angels who punished the evil souls who resided there. The condemned included those who dishonored God, sinned against nature, and practiced enchantments and witchcraft. However, the rest of this heaven was an Eden-like garden where manna (a divine food) was made and the souls of the holy—those who were righteous and compassionate—resided. Angels of light watched over this heaven.

The fourth heaven, under the jurisdiction of archangel Michael, contained Holy Jerusalem and its temple, all made of gold, surrounded by rivers made of milk, honey, wine and oil. The Tree of Life was to be found in this heaven, as well as the sun and the moon. Here Enoch heard the singing of angels:

> In the midst of the heavens I saw armed soldiers, serving the Lord, with tympana and organs, with incessant voice, with sweet voice, with sweet and incessant *voice* and various singing, which is impossible to describe, and which astonishes every mind, so wonderful and marvelous is the singing of those angels, and I was delighted listening to it.

The fifth heaven was another prison, a fiery ravine where the angelic Watchers, or Grigori, were imprisoned for marrying into the human race (see "Rebel angels" later in this chapter).

The sixth heaven was full of scholarly angels, studying astronomy, nature, and *homo sapiens*. Here Enoch found archangels, as well as angels who ruled over all the cycles and functions of nature—the seasons, the calendar, the rivers and seas, the fruits of the earth, the grass, and so on. There also were angels who recorded all the lives and deeds of every human soul, to set forth before God.

In the seventh heaven, Enoch found the higher angels, such as the thrones, cherubim, seraphim and dominions, as well as "fiery troops of great archangels." These angelic host bowed down before the Lord, singing his praises.

Enoch's two angel guides left him at the end of the seventh heaven. He was terrified, but Gabriel appeared before him, caught him up as though a leaf caught up by wind, and transported him higher.

In the eighth heaven, called Muzaloth, Enoch saw the "changer of the seasons, of drought, and of wet, and of the 12 signs of the zodiac." The ninth heaven, called Kuchavim, holds the heavenly homes of the 12 signs of the zodiac.

Then archangel Michael escorted Enoch to the tenth heaven, where he held the face of God. It was, said Enoch:

> ...like iron made to glow in fire, and brought out, emitting sparks, and it burns.
>
> Thus I saw the Lord's face, but the Lord's face is ineffable, marvelous and very awful, and very, very terrible.
>
> ...And I cannot tell the quantity of his many instructions, and various voices, the Lord's throne very great and not made with hands, nor the quantity of those standing round him, troops of cherubim and seraphim, nor their incessant singing, nor his immutable beauty, and who shall tell of the ineffable greatness of his glory?

God instructed Michael to "take Enoch from out of his earthly garments, and anoint him with my sweet ointment, and put him into the garments of my Glory." Enoch then took on a shining appearance, like the angels around him. God summoned the archangel Pravuil, "whose knowledge was quicker in wisdom than the other archangels, who wrote all the deeds of the Lord," to bring out the books of knowledge for Enoch to read.

With Pravuil dictating, Enoch wrote 366 books in thirty days. He was then summoned by the Lord, who revealed to him the creation story, and that the world would end on the eighth day of creation (or after 8,000 years), when time would cease. Enoch was given all the rules of morality and righteousness for humans to live by.

After these revelations, Enoch was sent back to earth for 30 days, so that he could pass on the teachings to his sons and others. God then took Enoch back into heaven and transformed him into Metatron.

## The angelic hierarchy

Just as the Judeo-Christian concept of the cosmos is hierarchical, so is the arrangement of angelic beings that inhabit it. Borders blur, for angels sometimes occupy more than one position and play multiple roles simultaneously. Some are both good angels and fallen angels. For example, before the Fall, Satan was the ruler of the seraphim, the highest order of angels. At the same time, he was also considered an archangel, a position much lower on the totem pole.

The best-known hierarchy derives from the two main sources of information on the subject: Pseudo-Dionysius's *Celestial Hierarchies* and St. Thomas Aquinas's *Summa Theologica*.

Pseudo-Dionysius is a mysterious Greek figure credited with authoring some enduring theological and philosophical tracts. The name is a pseudonym, and the real identity of the person writing under it is unknown. He has been confused with Dionysius the Areopagite, a Biblical figure; hence the "pseudo" attachment to the name. He may have been a Syrian clergyman.

The exact dates of Pseudo-Dionysius's writings are unknown, but thought to date to the fifth or sixth centuries. The works were influential on medieval Christian thought, including St. Thomas Aquinas (1225-1274), one of the great theologians of the Middle Ages.

Pseudo-Dionysius followed the Platonic and Neoplatonic pattern of three. He conceived of all reality in triadic hierarchies. In *Celestial Hierarchies*, he presents an angelic kingdom divided into three realms, each of which contains three orders, each of which further is broken down into three levels of intelligences. In each group of three, the function of the first level is perfection or union. Of the second level, it is illumination, and of the third level, it is purification. This triadic arrangement provides a means for the divine, or spirit, to descend into matter, and for matter to ascend to divinity.

A hierarchy, said Pseudo-Dionysius, is "a sacred order, a state of understanding and an activity approximating as closely as possible to the divine." The goal of a hierarchy "is to enable beings to be as like as possible to God and to be at one with him." Thus, through the angelic hierarchy, humankind has a way of reaching up to God and sharing in the light that emanates from him.

Pseudo-Dionysius said that angels are nearer to God than are humans, "since their participation in him takes so many forms." He elaborated:

Their thinking processes imitate the divine. They look on the divine likeness with a transcendent eye. They model their intellects on him. Hence it is natural for them to enter into a more generous communion with the Deity, because they are forever marching towards the heights, because, as permitted, they are drawn to a concentration of an unfailing love for God, because they immaterially receive undiluted the original enlightenment, and because, ordered by such enlightenment, theirs is a life of total intelligence. They have the first and most diverse participation in the divine, and they, in turn, provide the first and most diverse revelations of the divine hiddenness. That is why they have a preeminent right to the title of angel or messenger, since it is they who first are granted the divine enlightenment and it is they who pass on to us these revelations which are so far beyond us.

At the center of the triadic angel kingdom is God, emitting rapid vibrations which slow as they move out from the source and become light. As the vibrations slow, they become heat and finally matter. Nine orders of celestial beings surround God, divided, as mentioned, into three triads. At any level, the higher angels possess all the powers of those lower, but not those of any higher level.

The upper triad is composed of seraphim (love), cherubim (knowledge), and Thrones (the carriers of God). The entities of the upper triad are in direct contact with God. They receive "the primal theophanies and perfections," said Pseudo-Dionysius, which they pass on to the middle triad. The middle triad consists of dominions, powers and virtues. They in turn pass the word to the last triad, which is home to principalities, archangels, and finally angels. This last triad is responsible for communicating God's word to humans. Here are more details about each level:

## Seraphim

Their name means "fire-makers" or "carriers of warmth." The seraphim establish and hold the vibration of love, which in turn creates the field of life. These angels are of such subtlety that they rarely are perceived by human consciousness. When they so choose, they can manifest in a human-like form with four heads and six wings—two for flying, two to cover the face and two to cover the feet. They are able to shed their skin and appear in their true, brilliant form. They are often identified with the serpent or dragon.

Enoch declared that there are only four seraphim, one for each direction.

### Cherubim

The name comes from the Hebrew *kerub*, which means either "fullness of knowledge" or "one who intercedes." Their name, said Pseudo-Dionysius, "signifies the power to know and see God, to receive the greatest gifts of his light, to contemplate the divine splendor in primordial power, to be filled with the gifts that bring wisdom and to share these generously with subordinates as a part of the beneficent outpouring of wisdom." Cherubs have four faces and four wings. They also function as charioteers to God.

### Thrones

Thrones function as the actual chariots driven by the cherubs. They are depicted as great wheels containing many eyes, and reside in the area of the cosmos where material form begins to take shape. They chant glorias to God and remain forever in his presence. They are equated with ophanim and galgallin, angels mentioned in other hierarchies.

### Dominions

Dominions (also known as "dominations," "lords" and "kuriotetes") regulate the duties of the angels. They also function as channels of mercy.

### Powers

Also called "potentiates," "dynamis" and "authorities," these angels act as patrols, on the watch for demons trying to exert their evil influence. While they work to maintain a balance between good and evil, they themselves can be either good or evil. Camael is the ruler of the powers, and is a favored angel, but he is also known as a duke of hell. Either way, he rules 144,000 angels of vengeance and death. Powers also serve as spirit guides to the deceased who have lost their way.

*Virtues*
These beings are in charge of miracles and providing courage, and are sometimes referred to as "the shining ones" or the "brilliant ones."

*Principalities*
Principalities have "princely powers" and watch over the actions of the Earth's nations and cities. They are also in charge of religion on this planet.

*Archangels*
Archangels are a busy lot: they are liaisons between God and mortals; they are in charge of heaven's armies in the battle against hell; and they are the supervisors of the guardian angels.

Michael is the most famous of the archangels, and the only one to be named an archangel in the Bible. He is the angel who defeated Satan and hurled him into hell, and who will return with the keys to hell in order to lock him up for one thousand years. Michael is usually depicted carrying a sword and possessing "many-eyed" wings—that is, covered in peacock feathers. He possesses attributes of the Greco-Roman god Hermes/Mercury, given to him by the Church, which was attempting to convert the worshipers of that god. For example, he is known as the spirit guide of the dead, a job inherited from Hermes/Mercury.

Other angels have been accorded the rank of archangel. Gabriel is the angel of annunciation, resurrection, mercy, and death, and is the angel who appeared to Mary to inform her of her unusual pregnancy. Gabriel guides the soul from paradise to the womb and there instruct it for the nine months prior to birth. He has 140 pairs of wings and is said to sit at the left of God.

Raphael's name originates from the Hebrew term *rapha*, which means healer or doctor. Thus, Raphael is "the shining one who heals." He is often connected with the symbol of healing, the serpent. He is entrusted with the physical well-being of the earth and its human inhabitants, and is said to be the friendliest of the angels. However, he can also appear in the form of a monster and behave in a demoniacal manner.

Uriel is a punishing angel—the one who stood with fiery sword at the gates of Eden. He also punished Moses for not circumcising his son. But Uriel is not without a compassionate side. He gave the Kabbalah mystical teachings to humanity, and warned Noah of the coming flood.

*Angels*

The higher beings closest to the material world are the angels. They are the true couriers of the heavens, delivering the messages of God to humans. Angels also are the musicians of the cosmos. The vibrations of their music are more spiritual impulses than sound waves; thus it is not heard by humans as music but experienced as moods and inspirations.

## Rebel angels

To err may be human, but we aren't the only ones capable of making bad decisions. Most angel lore contains stories of angels gone bad. According to the Bible, one-third of heaven's legion fell from grace—figuratively and, according to some legends, literally.

As previously mentioned, Enoch witnessed a penal colony in the fifth heaven where gigantic angels known as the Grigori (or Watchers, or Those Who Sleep Not) were kept prisoner. About 200 Watchers, who were assigned to watch over the earth—became entranced with human women. They decided to disobey God, descend to Earth, and take the women as wives. This act had many problematic consequences. It was a sin of hubris—a mixture of pride and lust. It also resulted in a mixing of the spiritual with the material, which was strictly forbidden by God. In exchange for sex, the Watchers gave humans secret angelic knowledge on growing herbs, working with minerals, working enchantments, and so on.

Worse still, the union between the fallen angels and the daughters of Eve resulted in unnatural offspring: the Nephilim, or "fallen ones," who were gigantic, destructive creatures. They required great amounts of food, and when it ran out they ate humans and even turned on each other. God was so enraged by the bloodshed and corruption that he sent the Flood to cleanse the earth. However, there was a second occurrence of these creatures in Canaan, and Israel was charged with destroying them. The destruction was incomplete, and many got away, their fate unknown.

The Watchers fared worse. They were rounded up by archangels and imprisoned forever. Their leader, Azazel, was cast by Raphael into a dark pit (either in the Earth or in the fifth heaven), where he will remain until Judgment Day, when he will be cast into the fire.

Free will has gotten other angels into trouble. A legend of the Fall tells of a war between free-willed angels, some who were fortified by the grace of God and some who were on their own. Those with God's extra shot of grace, led by archangel Michael, defeated the army of 133 million and cast them down to hell.

St. Thomas Aquinas stated that the angels' only opportunity for free will is at the time of their creation, and even then, they always choose God. However, the Gnostics believed that, in exercising their free will, angels naturally drifted away from God. The angels who drifted the least stayed in the astral plane; those who drifted the farthest became demons.

The most infamous of the rebel angels is Lucifer, the Bringer of Light turned Prince of Darkness, who is usually credited with leading the other angels in the big Fall. Lucifer is identified as Satan (from the heavenly office of *ha-satan*, or adversary), who, while still in the heavens, appeared to hold more than one position in the hierarchy simultaneously. Similarly, he possessed a multitude of aliases and personalities. He made a colossal blunder of pride and was condemned forever to a dark, embittered existence. Lucifer lost his luminous quality and inherited the goat-like features of his randy Greek ancestor, Pan.

Perhaps it was Satan's refusal to bow to Adam when God presented him to the angels. One legend has it that Satan refused to bow because he had been previously instructed to bow to no one but God. He was just obeying orders. Perhaps he refused to bow to any but God because of his deep love for the Creator. Or, perhaps he was jealous of God's creation, which explains his continuing efforts to separate humankind from God. Regardless, Lucifer was flung into hell, and one-third of the angels followed him.

In another legend, Lucifer was Shaher, the Morning Star, the last star to leave the sky before the sun rose. One morning, his pride got the best of him and he tried to overcome the rising sun; for this act of insubordination he was expelled from heaven.

### Gnostic angelology

The Gnostics were a mystical Christian sect that flourished in the second century. They believed that matter is evil and that freedom comes from *gnosis*, or spiritual truth. The Church considered them heretical, and persecuted and purged them.

One of the Gnostics' acts of heresy was their disagreement over the Judeo-Christian theory of creation. Gnostics said there was no singular, higher being who created the world. Rather there was an all-encompassing divine spirit which divided itself, creating various worlds and beings, human and spiritual, in the process. One of these was the female principal Sophia, who represented the concept of Wisdom. Other emanations from the source included the concepts of love, power, truth, and mercy. These formless concepts eventually solidified into angelic beings.

At one point, the divine source withdrew itself from these beings and gave them the free will to stay or to go. Some chose to remain close to the source, serving it and aiding those humans who desired reunion with the divine. Others—the fallen angels—became so alienated from the source that they grew arrogant, all claiming themselves to be the One and Only. According to the Gnostics, the Creator who is worshipped in Judeo-Christian religions is actually one of these arrogant fallen angels. Satan falsely claimed to be the creator and ruler of the cosmos, and we believed him.

### Angelic beings in other religions

Religions and cultures that do not embrace the Judeo-Christian concept of angels believe in intermediary spiritual beings who act as mentors and guardians.

While the angels of Western religions are a species genetically distinct from humans, the divine beings of Eastern religions are often humans who have reached a high rung on the karmic ladder. For example, Buddhist devas are mortal beings who have earned a place in the astral plane not accessible by regular human beings; however, being mortal, they are subject to the laws of reincarnation.

In Mahayana Buddhism, the *bodhisattvas* are humans who have attained enlightenment and total compassion. They reside between heaven and Earth, and like devas, must also pass through the cycle of reincarnation. The spiritual energy within them is referred to as a *dakini*, or angel. Bodhisattvas act in the usual angelic capacity toward humans, teaching and healing; they also guide the spirits of the dying.

In Taoism, the Immortals are former humans who have attained physical immortality and status as demi-gods. They fulfill angelic-like duties of healing, protecting, and delivering messages.

In Hinduism, bird-like *apsaras* carry the dead into paradise.

Candomble emphasizes communion with nature as the path to guidance and enlightenment. Humans can receive truth and wisdom by approaching the spirits of nature with an attitude of humility and good intentions. The angel-like beings of this religion are known as *orishas*, immaterial beings who act as helpers to Olorun, the god of Candomble. Each is aligned with an element of nature, much like the Hindu devas. Chango, for example, is the *orisha* of thunder, and Oshoun, the *orisha* of romantic love and fertility. They make up a family of more than 400 members, with Oshala as the father of orishas and Yemanja as the mother.

The energy of the *orishas* is dualistic; thus, there are both male and female spirits. At birth everyone receives a male and a female *orisha*, which behave in the manner of guardian angels. In order to discover the identities of one's *orishas* and receive their guidance, a person must go to a "power spot," a place in nature where one feels most at peace and attuned to the cosmos. When a person intuitively discovers power spots, he or she discovers the home of the personal *orishas*, and it is there that their guidance can best be received.

Native Americans have angel-like creatures in animal form, spirits who help people and deliver divine messages. Shamans, in their visits to the underworld, are accompanied by animal spirit guides. Many Indian cultures believe that the spirits of their ancestors act as guardian angels to the living.

**Cycles of popularity**
Angels reached a height of popularity during the Middle Ages. They experienced an explosion in population and power, being everywhere and protecting all things, and their estimated numbers soared to over three hundred million.

What goes up must come down, even angels. Various historical events contributed to their loss in popularity. The Inquisition focused attention away from the angels to demons. The Black Plague diminished people's faith in celestial protectors.

By the end of the Renaissance, interest in angels was at a low point as spiritual contemplation was replaced by a new focus on science. The Age of Enlightenment arrived. Knowledge, formerly a privilege of the Church, became more available through the invention of the printing press. Astronomical discoveries put Earth in its place: a tiny dot in an overwhelmingly large cosmos. Angels disappeared from serious discussion, and in the art world they were replaced by pagan gods.

The Protestant Reformation of the sixteenth century deemphasized the Christian angel hierarchy and emphasized the fallen angels and their leader. John Calvin denounced the consideration of angels to be a waste of time. Martin Luther acknowledged the existence of angels, but said they were not divine and should be kept in "proper" perspective.

The Church has vacillated on the subject of angels over the centuries. Saint Paul denounced the worship of angels. In 325 the Council of Nicea, which decided the core of Christian theology, acknowledged the existence of angels. In 343 another church council said they should not be worshipped. By the end of the eighth century, archangels were accepted to a limited extent, and their names and duties agreed upon. In the first half of the twentieth century, popes Pius XI and XII were vocal champions of guardian angels.

Today, angels and guardian angels are part of Catholicism, and play valuable roles in the spiritual growth of people.

### Angels today

Angels have survived the peaks and valleys in their popularity. Whenever people feel in need of spiritual help, they look to intermediary beings for assistance. In times of widespread turmoil—war and conflict, economic failures, and natural disasters—angels are called upon.

# 3

# The Changing Image of Angels

Angels are incorporeal, but have the ability to assume form. Some of the Biblical angels are earthy and humanoid, such as the three strangers who enjoyed Abraham's hospitality. The angel found sitting inside Christ's tomb was man-like as well. Other Biblical angels were described as human-like but with an unearthly radiance, or mysterious beings, such as the entities seen by the prophet Ezekiel. Winged creatures descended in a fiery cloud, and had four faces each: human, ox, eagle, and lion). They moved on wheels and made a tremendous thundering noise.

After the Council of Nicea admitted angels into the emerging dogma of the Christian Church, theologians engaged in heated debates over whether or not angels could, or even should, be depicted in art. The Church inherited descriptions but no images of angels from Judaism. Some Christian theologians argued that beings of spirit could not be adequately and accurately portrayed in art, and, furthermore, images would encourage idolatry. The disputes became bitter, and were an important factor in the division between Western and Eastern orthodoxies.

Artists in the Western Church first turned to pagan gods such as Nike, Eros, and Hermes as models for angels, giving them wings that were small and grew in size over the centuries. Halos and shining lights around angels appeared in art by the end of the fourth century.

During the Renaissance, angels took on more human-like, fleshy appearances. Artists used adolescent boys and swan wings as models. Angels looked more like beautiful human beings than beings made of spiritual energy. The cherubim were reduced to chubby infants modeled on Italian *putti*, funerary figures, images that are still popular today.

By the end of the Renaissance, artists, like the rest of society, lost interest in angels. Victorian era angels continued the Renaissance form. Sad and somber angels were used as tomb monuments, and sweet, feminine angels depicted guardian angels.

Modern angel art portrays angels in many forms, including Renaissance style, icons, and abstract forms.

## What are angels made of?

The substance of angels has been much debated through history. St. Thomas Aquinas said that angels are intellect without substance. They are pure thoughtforms. However, they can take on a physical body if they wish and if it makes their jobs easier.

Swedish mystic Emmanuel Swedenborg, in the eighteenth century, through his personal communications with angels, discovered that angels have no material body and therefore cannot reflect light and be visible. They can only be seen if they take on a body temporarily, or by being perceived through the inner eye, or third eye. They are capable of speech, Swedenborg said, using consonants to express ideas and vowels to express love.

Our many experiences of angels throughout the ages indicate that angels appear in whatever form is appropriate for each situation. However, we relate to them best as spiritual mirrors of ourselves, reflecting an idealized form.

## Angels and gender

Angels can appear as human-like men and women, but do they have their own gender? The Church states that angels are immaterial and therefore do not have reproductive abilities. In the Bible, God created angels before humans, and they do not go about reproducing themselves.

However, exceptions exist. For example, the Watchers—if they were indeed angels—had the ability to cohabit with human women and produce offspring. Christian theologians also allowed for the sexual abilities of demons, the fallen angels, used to torment humans.

Many people who have spontaneous experiences of angels have impressions of gender, such as one shared by Sharon C. of Santa Fe, Texas:

> I was lying on my back in bed when I awoke. My eyes surprisingly were already open when I realized the vision before me. It was hanging above my bed. I remember it so clearly. Especially the face. Its look was androgynous, but I felt that the gender was male. His features were plain and his skin pale. His hair was coarse blond with a layered look, but not too long. He was smiling at me.
>
> I thought that I might be having a narcoleptic seizure or something, but I leaned up on one arm to get closer. I asked him what he wanted. He just continued to smile at me. Maybe I should have asked him something different, because shortly after that he disappeared, leaving me staring at the ceiling.
>
> I never felt frightened or upset. My demeanor was calm and serene. I laid back in bewilderment, wondering what it was all about. I never doubted what I saw.

Sometimes angels appear to make us aware that they are present in our lives.

## Angels and eating

Another question that has stirred up theological debate over the centuries is whether or not angels eat food. In Genesis 18, the three angels who visit Abraham disguised as men sit down and eat with him. Did they actually consume food, or just give the appearance of doing so? In the book of Tobit, the archangel Raphael, who goes about disguised as a man, said that he caused people to have visions of him eating and drinking in order to disguise his identity.

**Our own perceptions**

Angels do whatever suits their mission and purpose—but we also create their appearances and behavior through our beliefs and projections. Angels are vibrations of love and light—they are truly formless. In order for us to be able to perceive them, and to comprehend them, we ourselves project shape, features and identities onto them, based on our needs of the moment, and our beliefs and cultural conditionings.

In times of great crisis, we may be so stressed that the appearance of a supernatural being would exacerbate our dilemma rather than alleviate it. Thus, angels appear to us as "real" human beings—the mysterious stranger, who appears suddenly and vanishes just as abruptly.

Kathryn C. of Chicago had an encounter with an angelic mysterious stranger, who communicated an important reminder to her about her lifestyle. Kathryn has been sensitive to supernatural forces since childhood, and has had various experiences with them. Angels often give her guidance through synchronicities, and through other people. The incident with the mysterious stranger occurred after she had spent a weekend concentrating on "matters unseen and unlimited."

> I was driving back home, a sixteen-hour drive with visits to friends along the way. It was a brilliant day and I stopped at a restaurant for a sandwich. As I was paying my bill, I saw behind the counter, on the wall, a larger-than-life-size relief of a figure of a sort of happy-go-lucky bum. It was part of this particular restaurant's theme, meaning the vagabond life on the road. This stylized bum had large, black, bulbous-tipped shoes with a big hole in the toe. As I was paying, I was thinking about how romanticized the 'life of a bum' was depicted, and the chances were than no 'real' bum would be eating in a place like that, as it would be too expensive.
>
> Well, I was on the road thinking about the weekend intensive, enjoying the brilliant day, thinking about the bum that was depicted on the wall. Later, I stopped to get something to eat at a fast food burger place, a quick stop off the interstate. When I ordered, I was the only person there, except for a *bum* who came in and stood next to me

and placed an order. One thing that caught my attention was that he was very soft-spoken and was grinning the whole time. He was not disheveled, just wasn't the year's fashion pick.

He asked if they had pineapple juice. No? Well, they should. And did they have yogurt? No? They should. The young woman behind the counter was amused and slightly bewildered. I thought this guy must come in often, as she seemed to be handling the situation very well.

He finally ordered something and pulled out a crisp twenty-dollar bill! It was very curious. But the one thing that stopped me cold in my tracks was, when I glanced down at his shoes, I saw the very shoe, with the hole in the toe that I had seen in the earlier restaurant.

The significance of what he tried to order first was this: at the time, I was going through some medical changes, and I know from dietary readings and research and my own experience that the acid-alkaline balance is very important to our body's system. Pineapple juice and yogurt would help set that balance up. And this 'bum' standing there ordering reminded me of my own health system concerning the acid-alkaline balance, and how yogurt and juice, so to speak, saved my life once.

Now, was this an angel? There were no wings. I know it wasn't a hallucination. He didn't talk to me directly, face to face, but I heard everything he said. I left and couldn't find him. I wanted to talk to him. Yet, at the same time I felt I got the message, and I felt a little strange, as I was by myself. I also could have asked the girl behind the counter a question or two, but didn't. Since then, I went to that first restaurant when I was in the area. They have changed their decor. What a shame.

I have always felt a strong sense of guidance and protection in my life. I still have an old, slightly crumbling picture with a large gilt frame, that hung over my bed during my youth, of a small boy and girl near a cliff with a large, kind, blue-and-white guardian angel gently guiding them away from danger. To me, these experiences and others have always represented spirits and guidance— angels, if you will. As I have matured, I have come to an understanding of them as not an outer force impinging some bizarre manifestation on me, but rather a response to some powerful *need* I have *in* me.

An angel as a "bum"? Had the mysterious stranger appeared in any other guise, he would not have had the same impact on Kathryn.

Angels also can masquerade as legendary figures and spirits of the dead. In certain situations, a person might resist communication with a supernatural being, but would be open to communication with a departed love one.

For Steve, angels appeared in the form of children when he faced potentially serious health problems:

Several years ago, I drove my car to a doctor's office to review laboratory test results drawn from my blood. This was a very serious condition, and as I sat in the parking lot, my body felt heavy and slightly dull from fear and tension. I did not look forward to the ten-minute walk from the parking lot to the doctor's office, where we would review the test results together.

While still seated in the car, I suddenly became aware of the presence of little children. They were all around me in the interior of the car. While I did not 'see' these children (aged five to twelve years) in the conventional sense through my eyes, I was aware of their various shapes, sizes and faces through an intuitive faculty or inner eye. As one might imagine, I immediately delighted in their presence and my spirits were uplifted.

We all got out of the car together and began walking towards the elevators in the attached office building where the doctor's office was. Two little girls walked by my side and held my hand, and perhaps another eight or ten were holding onto my arms, in a sense collectively supporting me as we walked. There was a sense of mirth and laughter, and I was consciously aware of the presence of these blessed creatures, though I am sure they were invisible to the eyes of others who may have been in that same physical space at the time.

They let me know they were the orphaned children of God and that they were here to cheer me and support me. Knowing that I would soon arrive at the doctor's office, I fought back the urge to cry in joy and relief, and settled instead for the blissful, teary-eyed gratitude of their presence.

As we entered the doctor's office, we all walked up to the receptionist's window to check me in for the appointment. They were still with me, though we all knew we would keep our little secret from others. These divine creatures remained with me. Even now I think back fondly of the children, and immediately connect with their omnipresent energy.

It is clear to me that the Divine Will desired that I remain in physical form and in good functional health. As in all matters, I say to our Beloved Creator, 'Thy Will Be Done.'

Our concepts of angels are influenced by thousands of years of historical description and comment, which have imbued certain images into our collective psyche. Yet, as the modern experiences show, angels mutate to fit modern ideas, environments and situations. When we are increasingly receptive to the presence of angels, and their ability and availability to interact in our lives, then less and less stage clothing will be necessary. Perhaps the ideal image of an angel is none at all, but a spiritual presence or force with which we commune via an inner knowing or awareness.

# 4

# Guardian Angels

The notion of a wise spirit looking out for our welfare is a comforting one. Guardian spirits of all kinds populate mythologies and religions. They guard places, people, and the cosmos. Guardian beings accompany people throughout their entire lives, and even lifetimes to lifetimes.

Philosopher Rudolf Steiner said every person has one guardian angel, who has a complete overview of that person's present and previous lives. This view of the big picture gives the angel knowledge of what experiences are necessary in the person's destiny, and it guides the person accordingly. It is limited in its ability to help, however, by its charge's belief in the angel. If the person recognizes the existence of the angel, then the wheels of celestial guidance are greased.

The Gnostic guardian angel took the form of the "twin angel." All people, according to this belief, have an enlightened spirit attached to them—their celestial twin. Some Gnostics believed that only very advanced people could communicate with their angel, and most had to wait until death to be united. However, Gnostic prophet Valentinus proposed that anyone could contact their twin angel through a rite known as the "bride chamber." In this mystery rite, the human twin is the bride, the angel twin is the groom, and the wedding is the journey of human consciousness into the astral plane.

The Bible supports the concept of guardian angels. In Exodus, Moses is sent an angel to guard him. Psalms 91:11-13 states:

> He will give his angels charge of you to guard you in all
> your ways. On their hands they will bear you up, lest you
> dash your foot against a stone. You will tread on the lion
> and the adder, the young lion and the serpent you will
> trample under foot.

In the book of Tobit, Raphael, in the guise of a mortal man, accompanies young Tobias on a journey, advises him, guides him, and teaches him magical and healing arts.

In Catholicism, there are movements devoted to the cult of the guardian angel. Like saints and the Virgin Mary—who also have cults within the Church—guardian angels offer an important means to bring human beings closer to God. St. Bernard said that it is our duty to love, respect and trust our guardian angels, and this has become part of the Catholic Church's liturgy.

Angels are not mentioned directly in the Creed in the Mass, which proclaims belief in "one God, the Almighty maker of heaven and earth, of all that is, seen and unseen." The Council of Trent (1545-1563) declared that "heaven and earth" encompassed everything contained in heaven and earth, including the angels.

How many guardian angels does a person have? One, according to the Church, although persons with important positions in government are given two: one for them, one for their position. However, one of the early fathers of the Christian church, Origen, wrote that each person has two guardian angels, a good one and a bad one. Like the Greek *daimones*, the good angels attempt to steer people in the right direction, and the bad angels try to lead them astray.

My own belief is that everyone has multiple angels around them, all serving different needs and stages of growth. Some angels are present from birth to death and beyond, and others come and go as life progresses.

Guardian angels are as influential as we allow them to be. The more we believe in them and call on them, the greater their presence and influence in our lives. St. Thomas Aquinas said angels are able to intervene in our lives because they possess a vastly superior knowledge of the natural universe, as well as a mysterious power over the material world. Thus, what they are capable of doing seems miraculous to us. In addition, they can act on our senses, inspire us and strengthen our minds, causing us to see our situations more clearly, Aquinas said. Merely coming into contact with angels makes us better persons. In effect, believing in them liberates our higher selves and our greater creative potential.

Pope Pius XI (r. 1922-39) was on particularly good terms with his guardian angel, praying to him every morning and evening, and in between, if a day was rough. Pius XI did not hesitate to acknowledge this publicly, and even recommended the same to others. He confided to the man who someday would be pope himself, Monsignor Angelo Roncalli (John XXIII), that angels helped him in his many delicate diplomatic dealings. Prior to a meeting with someone whom Pius XI needed to persuade, he would pray to his guardian angel, recommending his argument, and asking him to take it up with the guardian angel of the other person. Sometimes Pius XI would himself invoke the guardian angel of the other person, asking to be enlightened as to the other's viewpoint.

Pius XI's experiences influenced John XXIII (r. 1958-63), who also maintained a deep and abiding faith in guardian angels. He used his radio addresses to exhort followers never to neglect devotion to their guardian angels, who stood ready at all times to help. He particularly urged parents to educate their children that they were not alone, but always in the company of their guardian angels. Like Pius XI, John XXIII sought the help of the guardian angels of those with whom he had difficulties. Even if no difficulties were present, John XXIII always acknowledged and paid respect to all guardian angels present at any meeting or gathering. He often acknowledged to his secretary how his guardian angel had inspired him to do various things, and had given him the idea to call an ecumenical council.

Pius XII (r.1939-58) did not confide his own personal dealings with angels, but did publicly support belief in angels. In an encyclical in 1950, he said it is a mistake to question whether angels are "real beings," and that this error in thinking could undermine church doctrine. He urged people to renew their devotion to angels. In 1958, a few days before his death, he gave an address to a group of American tourists, in which he reminded them of the existence of an invisible world populated with angels:

> Everyone, no matter how humble he may be, has angels to watch over him. They are heavenly, pure and splendid, and yet they have been given to us to keep us company on our way: they have been given the task of keeping careful watch over you so that you do not become separated from Christ, their Lord.
>
> And not only do they want to protect you from the dangers which waylay you throughout their journey: they are actually by your side, helping your souls as you strive to go ever higher in your union with God through Christ.
>
> ...We do not want to take leave of you...without exhorting you to awaken, to revive your sense of the invisible world which is all around us...and to have a certain familiarity with the angels, who are forever solicitous for your salvation and your sanctification. If God wishes, you will spend a happy eternity with the angels: get to know them here, from now on.

In 1968, Pope Paul VI sanctioned the Opus Sanctorum Angelorum ("the Work of the Holy Angels"), a movement intended to renew and bolster belief in guardian angels, and to foster a collaboration between angels and humans for the glory of God, the salvation of humanity, and the regeneration of all creation. There are three phases in the Opus.

In the first phase, initiates make a promise to God that they will love their guardian angels and will respond to their instructions when heard through the voice of conscience. This phase lasts for one year.

In the second phase, the initiates participate in a candlelight ceremony in the presence of the Blessed Sacrament, in which they consecrate themselves to their "holy guardians." They pledge to become like angels, and to venerate angels, who have been given to humanity by God "in a very special way in these days of spiritual combat for the Kingdom of God."

In the third phase, the initiate participates in a ceremony of consecration to all the angel kingdom.

The Opus brings to life powerful psychic forces in the individual, thereby facilitating the release of tremendous creativity in all areas of life.

Many people wonder why, if guardian angels are supposed to protect us, bad things happen in life. Why is one person saved from a tragic accident by the intervention of an angel, and another person is not?

Tragedies and difficulties do not happen because angels desert us. Angels are always with us. For reasons of spiritual and karmic growth, which we may not always be able to fully comprehend, we must at times go through pain. Some individuals have a hard road, while others glide through life blessed by few difficulties. Perhaps these circumstances are decided upon at a very high level of consciousness prior to coming into the world. However, whenever we are confronted with problems, angels are ready to help us cope. Pain provides opportunities for spiritual growth. Angels are not empowered to make decisions for us about our life's plan. They can only intervene under circumstances that may not be readily apparent to us, if ever completely understood. Angels also can provide a source of spiritual nourishment when we most need it.

**Names**
The Bible alludes to myriads and myriads of angels, yet only two are named: Michael and Gabriel. (The book of Tobit, which is included in the Catholic canon, names a third, Raphael.) With so many anonymous angels floating about, is it necessary to find names for them? When we come into awareness of our own guardian angels, do we have to call them by a name? The early Hebrews believed in a complex hierarchy of angels, all with their own names. In mystical Judaism, names have great significance, and manifest various powers.

Naming is important: it defines, and invests life, power, and potential. Without names, we cannot call out to specific "addresses" in the higher planes, or invoke beings, forces and energies into our own dimension.

Mystical, spiritual, magical, and fraternal orders have initiation rituals in which the initiate takes on a new name, usually secret, as a personification of his or her rebirth into the order. The name signifies new powers, new knowledge, and higher spiritual attainment.

William G. Gray, author of some of the most respected contemporary works on the Western mystery tradition, stated in *Inner Traditions of Magic*:

> The purpose behind the principle of naming anyone or anything at all, is to direct and hold the energy of Consciousness in some particular way at some especial point or portion of Existence. It is essentially an act of co-creation, and therefore Magical. Humanity gives names to whatever exists, while Divinity gives Existence to whatever is Named. When a human being 'utters a name,' the object of that name has its primary existence only in their own mind or 'imagination.' When Divinity Utters a Name, Existence manifests wherever it is intended, even in material form, because everything including ourselves is 'in the imagination of God.' And *that* is far beyond the imagination of Man.

Thus, discovering one's guardian angel is like initiation into an order. When we name angels, a gateway opens to higher levels of consciousness, and the angel's name is the password. The name gives us access, and provides us safety as we navigate these higher realms. Naming the guardian angel is one of the most important parts of the Opus Sanctorum. Angelorum.

One of the best ways to discover the name of a guardian angel is to ask for it in prayer or meditation. The name will arise spontaneously in your thoughts.

Jayne Howard Feldman, an author and channeler of angels—and creator of Be An Angel Day—agrees on the importance of naming one's guardian angel:

> The greatest gift you can give to God and the angels is that you believe," she said. "By giving an angel a name, you make an offering to God that yes, you believe. You believe in God's kingdom, and you believe in the wonderful being you are going to name. The name creates a rapport and makes it easier for you to communicate. Angels are going to do their work no matter what we call them.

They themselves don't bother with names. But, there will always be a message in the angel's name that comes to you, perhaps relating to your own gifts.

## Discovering LNO

Alma Daniel, an interfaith minister and healer in New York City, established a close connection to her angels, including her guardian angel, in the mid-1980s. Their involvement in her life profoundly influenced her own spiritual growth, her outlook on life, her ability to handle difficulties—and her own work helping others. She is co-author, with Timothy Wyllie and Andrew Ramer, of *Ask Your Angels*, a handbook for tuning into the angelic presence via meditation, dreams and visualizations.

In an interview I had with her at her New York City apartment, Alma shared her angel experiences and insights. I was greeted by a lovely atmosphere of serenity and peace, the results of working with the beautiful energies of angels.

"For most of my life, I didn't believe in angels," Alma said. "I thought they existed somewhere, but I didn't really feel there was an angel for me. That was for other people. I think many people feel that way, maybe there are angels, but they don't have one themselves.

"So, for years I was more in the mind and not so much in the spirit. Then I began studying a variety of teachers and healers, and understood that there was more than just this life and just this person, that there were other forces. But I didn't come into contact with angels until I was in a relationship with a man, Timothy Wyllie, who was very, very dear to me. H was a firm believer in angels, and he kept saying, 'I know you've got an angel, in fact I can sense your angel's presence.' I kept saying back that I didn't feel it and didn't believe it.

"Then, in 1985, I got sick with the flu. A lot of trouble had gone down in my life, and sometimes when you have a lot of trouble, you get sick because you just need time to reflect. I was in bed and was looking through some old notebooks that I had kept of various workshops and training that I'd attended to raise my consciousness. I ran across a record of a training I'd done seven years earlier, in which I was asked to visualize a lovely space, to wait for the arrival of my spirit guides and to welcome them when they came. According to my notes, I got two guides. One was a guy in purple tights and an Elizabethan doublet. His name was Greg. I remember thinking at the time, gosh, he's not my type at all. The other was a woman who looked like she was from the 1940s. She had a pompadour hairdo, and her hair was in a snood, and she was wearing a broad-shouldered, checked suit. She said her name was Eleanor. I thought, 'Eleanor reminds me of my mother, and this couldn't be my guide.' I forgot about the whole experience.

"Timothy came into the room to bring me a cup of tea. He said, 'Your angel is right here now. I can feel her presence. Just ask for her name.'

"I said, 'If you're so smart, *you* ask for her name.' He closed his eyes, and within a moment, he said, 'Elena.' I said, 'No.' I told him the story about the workshop and how Eleanor had come in. I thought it was a common name, and I wasn't going to deal with a common name like that, and Elena sounded just like Eleanor with his English accent.

"Timothy said, 'Okay, you do it. *You* get your angel's name.'

"I said, 'I can't!' He said, "All you do is shut your eyes and ask.'

"So I slammed my eyes shut and asked for the name of my angel. On the back of my forehead, I saw the letters L-N-O: Eleno. Chills went through my body, because I realized that she had tried to come in to me seven years earlier, and I heard the name Eleanor. And Timothy got the name Elena. And when I asked, it wasn't a name as we would call a name, but it was letters, L-N-O. I was totally convinced! Timothy told me to ask her questions, and I started writing down what she was saying. It was something I really didn't want to hear, so I knew that I wasn't making it up.

"From that point on, I've made regular contact with LNO. I do that just by closing my eyes and calling to her, and asking her a question. She will come in and I will write down the answer. Basically, it's channeling.

"Several months later, Timothy and I decided that we needed to put this information out in the world and show other people how to reach their own angels. We started a workshop called Opening to the Angels in December 1985. We asked the angels to bring in exactly the people who needed to be there, and thirty people showed up. We were not sure what we were going to do, but we opened ourselves to guidance, Timothy to his angels and I to my own, and we developed the GRACE process that later we followed."

"What is the process?" I asked.

"GRACE involves the basic steps of Grounding, Releasing, Aligning, Conversing, and Enjoying," explained Alma. "You center yourself, feel yourself present, release whatever negativity, doubt, fear or disappointment that you might have. We were given ways to attune to the angels, ways that people could tune their vibration up to establish a higher frequency so that they would be prepared to speak and to listen to the angels. This work involves the higher chakras: the throat, the heart, the third eye, and the crown. The angels guided us as we went along. We developed meditations in which we would take turns speaking. We never knew what was going to be said in advance, we just trusted."

Alma said she envisions LNO as female, though she doesn't believe that angels have genders. They have both male and female qualities, and present a dominant side to the person. She channels LNO in meditation, as well as at her computer. She always records what LNO tells her. Quite often, LNO breaks in when Alma is mildly distracted, such as when she is walking on the street, or engaged in some activity.

"About a year after my angel came in I was about to do a very large conference here in New York for float tanks," Alma said. "It was an enormous amount of work, and I was quite concerned about carrying all of it. As I was just walking along the street one day, LNO came in and said, 'Help will be given to you. Don't worry.' I trusted that, and I dropped the agitation I had about whether I was going to be able to be able to pull the conference off. Sure enough, people began appearing to help out with various things. It was a great success—a hundred people showed up from all over the world for this conference."

Alma said that often, LNO tells her things she would rather not hear. "I was in the middle of dissolving a relationship that I had been in. It was very painful, and I was at the stage of blame, making wrong, and feeling very disappointed. One day I was walking along the street, going to my exercise class, and LNO's voice came in and said, 'Nobody is doing anything to you. People just do what they do. It's the way you're taking it.' I thought, *Thanks a lot*! But it sparked in me the understanding that I was playing victim and I didn't need to.

"Sometimes people ask me to channel for them. I don't like to do that. I should say, LNO doesn't like to do that, because she feels people have the ability to do that themselves, and it's not good for them to rely on others. It's better for them to go within and to develop that capacity for themselves. Anybody can, you know, it's not given to the few or the chosen. It's an ability that we all have, to hear higher voices, to hear spirit, and to bring that into our lives.

"LNO is a voice, and she often refers to herself as 'we,' not as 'I.' She has told me that she's a voice in a collective of angels whose function is to connect people with their Higher Selves. That's specifically her function, to oversee everything that I do, so that if I bring her in, it's my higher Self that is operating at that point. Then I'm not coming from little self or little me. I'm coming from the higher view which is much more expansive."

"Do you hear Eleanor as an inner voice or an external voice?" I asked.

"Her voice is within me. There is a school of thought that says that angels are actually aspects of our Higher Selves. That's not a foreign concept to me. In other words, it could very well be that I've had to externalize part of myself and see it as coming from other than myself in order to give it the credence and the respect that I do. Maybe I wasn't prepared to give myself that, but I could give that to my Higher Self in the form of an angel."

"Do you experience other angels besides LNO?"

Alma nodded. "Sometimes other angelic presences come in for me as a feeling. The emotion is always a heart-opening, expanding love and tenderness and compassion. It is so palpably felt, Rosemary, the tears will come to my eyes and roll out of my eyes. I'm not sobbing, it's joyful. It's being in a place of such utter acceptance and love and compassion that, you know you're home.

"I don't see angels," she continued. "Other people are blessed in that kind of vision. I feel angels emotionally. I can feel it almost as a texture of changes in the air—it's a particular quality. Sometimes it's like silk, sometimes it's like velvet. But obviously these are other senses that I'm using. They're not my physical senses."

"What have your experiences led you to believe about the nature of angels?" I asked.

"The angel is a manifestation of God force. Just as we are a different manifestation of God force. Much of the time, we're not acting in a Godly way, but we have that capability within us. So, the angel is a reminder of who we really are, of a God within, of the divinity within us. The angel is also a particular source of comfort and reassurance. As people reach out to their angels, they begin to bring them more into the mainstream of their lives. The angel inspirits them. Now, the question is, are they being inspirited by the angel or are they just connecting to their own God spirit? I don't know, and I don't think it matters, because the outcome is the same—

human beings learning to be more human and more humane, not only to others, but to ourselves as well. It always seems easier to be good to other people than it is to be good to ourselves. When you really begin to dance with the angels and to live with the angels and to work, eat, and sleep with the angels, you take on a more loving way with yourself. Then, your contact with other people is vastly improved. Angels remind us about caring, about showing tenderness, and about showing respect."

"How can someone tell when they've contacted an angel? Is there a distinct feature to the voice or feelings involved?"

Alma said, "I've done a lot of work teaching people how to channel or contact their angels, and I'm always looking out for what's not an angel. The angel is never going to tell you, 'YOU DONE WRONG! YOU BAD!' The angel will approach whatever calamity or catastrophe you have created with a higher view, and will point out that you've chosen this or brought this into your life for the purpose of evolving and growing more in the light. If you get a transmission and it scolds you or criticizes you or tells you what to do, such as 'Move to Florida now,' don't trust that. It's not coming from your angel.

"I do make a distinction between angels and spirit guides. The spirit guide is generally a spirit that has been in physical form. Angels have never been in physical form. They've always been angels. Spirit guides can seem like angels to some people. However, they're concerned with the day-to-day life, while angels are much more concerned with uplifting your life to embrace the celestial—a knowing of greater realms, where values are quite different. The guides seem to have values which are of a very mundane level."

"Why is it so important for people to be more open to angels?"

"We're at a turning point of evolution, which, in terms of consciousness, is probably as great as the point in evolution when man first starting using his opposable thumb, discovered fire, and began to be a more conscious being," said Alma. "We're moving into a higher level of consciousness now, which is God consciousness. You're familiar with the idea that the Second Coming of Christ will be as a woman?"

I nodded.

"What that really means is that the feminine Christ consciousness is coming down now, into each one of us. It is the feminine principal that is being returned to the earth. The feminine principle represents the nurturer, the guardian and the caretaker. We need a return of this energy because we've been dominated by a patriarchy. As we move into this consciousness of the feminine Christ, we are beginning to develop and embody the feminine qualities of compassion, caring, forgiveness, and universal, unconditional love.

"We've had to be pushed to the very edge to get here. We've had to desecrate our mother, our home, our earth. We've had to pillage and abuse our brothers and sisters. The atrocities are incredible. We've got to know that it's within each one of us to be the bearers of light. That's why we need to connect with angels."

Alma said that being in touch with her guardian angel makes difficulties in life easier to bear and overcome. "Since the angel has come into my life, no matter what happens to me, I welcome it as a part of my growth, even though I might not like it. I know that if I embrace every experience, I will grow. My angel tells me that you will never finish your growth. She said that even after you leave the physical plane, you continue to evolve, though in a different way."

### Be An Angel Day

Our guardian angels may look after us on the mundane level, but one of their most important tasks is to help us grow spiritually, and that means inspiring us to be like angels to other people. Toward that end, the angels inspired Jayne Howard Feldman, whom I mentioned earlier in this chapter, to create Be An Angel Day. The angel holiday was launched on August 22, 1993.

Jayne is a woman of great talent who uses her gifts to help others, especially to help them develop their own ways of connecting to the angelic kingdom. She lives and works in the same area where she grew up, the rolling green countryside of Maryland. She founded a nonprofit charitable organization, Angel Heights, dedicated to spreading the work of angels. Jayne has been communing with angels since she was a teen. About a decade ago, she met a medium who informed her that she herself would soon begin to work as a medium. Jayne's gift opened up, and, with training and practice, she now is an open channel, which means she receives information from her angelic host all the time.

She clairvoyantly sees angels as ripples and waves of light around other people, and also has seen angels that have taken on human form.

Angels, Jayne said, "represent God. Angels can be everything and anything in order to inspire you, and to guide you and touch you."

The purpose of Be An Angel Day is service to others. The motto is 'Be an Angel, do one small act of service for someone, be a blessing in someone's life.' By doing this, said Jayne, we take on angelic energy ourselves.

The angels chose August because it is the eighth month of the year, which in numerology is the number of achievement, accomplishment and fulfillment, and is a master vibration number, the number of the Master Architect of all. Be An Angel Day is a project on a master level, the building of a bridge between two kingdoms.

The angels also directed Jayne to name The Angel Alliance as the official sponsor of Be An Angel Day. The Angel Alliance exists in spirit. "The name is symbolic of the alliance between the angelic kingdom and the human kingdom, and perhaps all other kingdoms--I'm sure everyone is involved with this—because they did not want to have any singular ego energy connected with Be An Angel Day," Jayne said. "The angels specifically did not want the day associated with any one person or organization, or to be a day of angel worship."

Be An Angel Day is about selfless service. "The angels bring a message that we are servants of God in our own life to achieve our highest good, and we can be servants and messengers to others, just like the angels are. Be An Angel Day encourages people to think about something they could do for someone. They will, in turn, take on angelic energy, and become a messenger and provide healing."

Every day should be Be An Angel Day, and in more ways than serving others. "There is a new realization taking place, a new form of thought," Jayne said. "We can hold an angelic vision. It involves people taking conscious responsibility for their own lives. The earth is a classroom. The 'aha' that we study for over many lifetimes is the understanding that we are one with God, and God resonates within our heart and inspires us toward the greatest good.

"Taking conscious responsibility for our lives means not blaming others for our problems, and deliberately deciding to learn and grow. People are turning inward and finding God within."

# 5

# How Angels Come Among Us

Angels have many ways of interacting with people, and their methods match the needs of the moment and the person.

**Direct intervention**
Benvenuto Cellini (1500-1571), an Italian goldsmith, sculptor and author, tells in his autobiography, *The Life of Benvenuto Cellini* (published posthumously in 1728) how an angel saved his life in prison. Cellini, a hotheaded man, was constantly engaging in scrapes and fights with other people. On several occasions, he was imprisoned, and was condemned to death. He was absolved once for murder, by Pope Paul III.

In 1535, Cellini was jailed in Rome on charges of stealing the jewels of Clement. Cellini was incarcerated high in the towers of the Castel Sant'Angelo. He made a daring attempt to escape by scaling down the castle walls on a rope made of bed sheets tied together. He was captured and thrown in the dungeon. While in the dungeon, he sank into despair and resolved to kill himself by hanging.

Just as he was about to hang himself, a tremendous invisible force knocked him back. An angelic youth appeared to him in a vision and lectured him about the importance of living. Cellini was released from the dungeon on the personal request of a cardinal. He went on to become one of the most celebrated artists of the Renaissance.

We've seen some other examples of how angels intervene directly in our lives, such as the invisible force that knocked Robert S. off the live wire, saving his life, and the pillar of light that appeared to Juliet Hollister.

Angels also intervene directly in the form of human beings. They are "mysterious strangers" who appear suddenly in times of distress. They know just what to do to solve someone's plight. Once the rescue has been made, they suddenly vanish. No one ever knows who they are.

Mysterious strangers can be male or female. Most often, they are male—usually a fresh-looking, clean-cut youth. They are usually well-dressed, polite, and knowledgeable about the crisis at hand. They speak, though sparingly, and they will even take physical hold of the people in distress.

Eileen Elias Freeman, author of several books on angels, including Touched By Angels, and is founder of the nonprofit AngelWatch Foundation. She has had many encounters with angels, including had a mysterious stranger angel after she was diagnosed with ovarian cancer. "I was devastated," Eileen said. "All the things I had believed about God's love and angels were about to go down the drain. The fallen angels capitalized on the situation, and I couldn't think straight for a while.

"Then a strange woman came into my life at a science fiction convention. She walked up to me and said, 'You're in trouble, dear, would you like to talk about it?' At the time, I was trying to convince myself that the doctors were wrong. We went to a restaurant. She told me things that changed the way I viewed the situation. She told me to trust in God, and to keep my eyes open for learning lessons, and to ask for help and take it wherever I could find it. She told me that healing would come, though not the kind I had in mind. She said I shouldn't beat myself over the head, and ask, why me?. Above all, she said, don't be afraid.

"I never asked her name. When I went to pay the bill, the waitress told me there would be no charge because the costume I was wearing was good. I said I would at least pay for the woman who was with me. The waitress said, "What woman?""

The night before her surgery, Eileen knew her life would be healed. She awoke and found herself out of her body, floating about three feet above her physical form, looking down upon it. "I felt so wondrously light," she said. "Everything around me was in colors. Then I saw a being of light who I knew was Raphael. He came and embraced my body as it lay on the bed and became one with me. I knew everything would be all right."

After a radical hysterectomy, Eileen was healed, and she has carried on the work of angels ever since.

One need not be in dire straits to have a mysterious stranger angel appear on the scene, as the following story from Linda A. of La Grange, Illinois, illustrates:

> I went into a local electronics store with my son, who had his newly purchased shortwave radio. He had been having difficulty receiving certain channels, and believed there was a problem with the radio. We began a discussion with the store manager. My son began to explain the problem, but the manager cut him off, trying to make it sound like my son didn't know how to operate the radio. The more my son tried to object, the more insistent the manager became.
>
> Suddenly, out of nowhere, this young man appeared at the register where we were standing, and intervened. He had something in his hand to purchase and said very quietly, yet with knowledge, that my son had a point. He proceeded to explain very calmly to the manager what the problem was. Not only did he solve the problem, but suddenly the manager was much nicer. Then the man purchased the item in his hand. It was *crystals* for a shortwave.
>
> I was just dumbfounded. The young man wished us a nice day and left the store. A couple of seconds later, I rushed out the door to thank him, but he was *gone*. He literally disappeared. The store is in the middle of the block, so you would still be able to see someone walking down the sidewalk. Obviously, this was not an ordinary human. I still get chills when I think about it.

The angelic "roadside rescue" is one of the most common forms of direct angelic intervention. In the roadside rescue, the mysterious stranger arrives to help the motorist stranded on a lonely road at night, or who is injured in an accident in an isolated spot. Or, human beings arrive just in the nick of time.

On August 4, 2013, a mysterious "angel priest" made world headlines concerning a near-fatal car crash. Katie Lentz, of Quincy, Missouri, was driving alone in her Mercedes early one Sunday morning on an isolated stretch of Highway 19 in Missouri when a drunk driver crashed head-on into her. The young woman was seriously injured and pinned in her mangled car. Rescuers arrived, blocked off the highway for a considerable distance, and went to work to free her. They labored for an hour without success. Meanwhile, Katie's vital signs dropped. At one point, she asked someone to pray for her. Suddenly, in the midst of the crowd of rescue workers, a voice said, "I will." Much to the amazement of everyone present, a Catholic priest had appeared out of nowhere. He offered a prayer and then gave the rescuers instructions on how to save Katie. Just as suddenly as the priest had appeared, equipment arrived that could pry the car apart and save the young woman. When rescuers looked around to thank the priest, he had vanished as mysteriously as he had arrived.

Even more amazing was the fact that the priest appeared in none of the photographs and videos taken on the scene. For several days, witnesses and others opined that they had indeed been visited by an angel in disguise. They described him as a silver-haired man in his 50s or 60s.

The mystery supposedly was solved about a week later when a real-life priest stepped forward and claimed responsibility. Silver-haired Reverend Patrick Dowling of Jefferson City, Missouri, said he was driving along the highway after mass when he saw the line of cars and blocked-off stretch of road. He stopped and went to give aid.

For some, that was the end of the matter—despite the fact that Dowling never explained how he got past the roadblocks forming a two-mile perimeter around the crash site. He would have had to walk a considerable distance, without being seen by a single person, in order to get to Katie's car.

There remain unanswered questions. Did the church put forward a priest to quell rising speculation in the media that a real angel had intervened? What harm is validation of the existence of God's messengers and agents? Dowling's diocese in Jefferson City remained silent. It seems that the church would like us to believe in angels—but not too much.

In my book *Christmas Angels: True Stories of Hope and Healing*, I document other stories of the sudden, unexpected appearance of an angelic mysterious stranger in times of crisis.

Jayne Howard Feldman is on the road around the world a great deal to lecture and give workshops. The angels have come to her aid a number of times, helping her avert accidents by instructing her what to do, or taking invisible control of the wheel or pedals. One night, the gas pedal in Jayne's car became stuck, and she ran off the freeway near Baltimore. She stopped the car by throwing the transmission into park. It would not restart, and she panicked. It was 10 PM and she was miles from the nearest exit. She prayed to the angels for help, and within minutes, a van pulled up, carrying a man and a woman. The woman rolled down her window and told Jayne not to be frightened, for they were Christians. Even so, many people would have been wary of strangers at night. But the angels gave Jayne assurances, and she accepted a ride to a gas station. She discovered that the couple lived in a town near hers, and knew her family. They pulled off to help Jayne, they said, because they had a daughter, and they hoped that if their daughter ever was in distress, she, too, would be aided.

**Prayer and meditation**

Prayer is a powerful way to commune with the Divine. Prayer directs psychic energy toward accomplishment. The noted healer, Ambrose Worrall (1899-1972), who practiced faith healing in Baltimore with his famous wife, healer Olga Worrall (1906-1985), once said that all thoughts are prayers. Thus, we should constantly strive to tune our thoughts to the highest expressions possible of love, benevolence and good will.

Angels listen to our thoughts and prayers. If you pray for their guidance, and are sincere and receptive, the guidance will be given.

Carol Ann D. a graphoanalyst in Clovis, New Mexico, told me about a prayer experience she had that evoked a church-full of angels. It occurred during a time when she was coping with family problems and the death of a friend. She went to evening mass to pray, but was so tired that she couldn't settle into her usual prayer, which was the mantra of "Jesus." Carol explained:

My concentration just wasn't there, so I started to say my mantra out loud. I was feeling down, not necessarily depressed, but world-weary. It seemed I couldn't do anything right at the time. I felt an urge to open Scripture. I had my little Gideon King James Bible with me in my purse, and I cracked it to Acts 4, verse 10. I was overjoyed when I read it, for it mentions the name of Jesus as healer. I felt approval at my efforts despite my weariness. I felt heard and acknowledged.

I was able to just settle down and pray when all of a sudden the whole church appeared to be filled up with moving light, flashes and singing. I felt like the angels, saints, seraphim and cherubim were all rejoicing with me and that the very universe, even the stones, sings praise when the name of Jesus is said or spoken. Don't ask me how, but I felt like the very name of Jesus is a caress to the Father, like a whisper of a kiss to his cheek. I can't tell you how long it lasted, or whether I saw with my open eyes. It felt like I did see with my eyes—the church was completely full of color, sounds, and movement, like it was going to burst open.

Carol called herself "a very ordinary questor." Her experience opened her up to many visions and insights, and she started teaching others how to meditate.

Alma Daniel has counseled people internationally on how to reach angels through meditation. "Sit in a quiet and peaceful place," she said. "Ground yourself and put your hand on your heart, which connects you to your own loving nature. Close your eyes and imagine the presence of your angel around you. How does that feel? Maybe you feel yourself being enclosed by these wonderful wings. Or maybe you feel yourself growing lighter. Whatever it is, acknowledge what you experience. Just stay with it. Notice how you're feeling, what your breathing is like. It's through the imagination that angels can come to us. If we can conceive of it, it can happen. Then ask the angel for its name. Or ask, 'Please be with me,' or 'Help me in this day.' Angels are here to help—they're not decorative. I ask for help in getting subway trains. I ask for help when I have to do a lot of errands. Now, I don't consider that my own guardian angel, LNO, handles these particular functions, but there are other angels that do so. And don't forget to say thank you!

"I always tell people to write down what they get. You'll know if it's your own thoughts. Quite often, angels tell us something we don't expect to hear, or don't want to hear. Communication also often comes in unbidden. You can't reach the angels willfully. You can only reach them through surrender. You can't command, 'NOW I WILL SPEAK WITH MY ANGEL! NOW!' Rather, you have to open yourself as a tool, an instrument for them to come through you. Always be grateful for the blessings in your life—it's a great pathway to angelic contact."

## Dreams

The Bible has some of the earliest stories about how angels appear to us in dreams. Genesis tells the story of Jacob, son of Isaac and Rebecca, who was hunted by his twin brother, Esau. Jacob escaped to his uncle. En route, he had a dream of angels ascending and descending a ladder to heaven. God promised him and his descendants the land upon which he slept. "I will not leave you until I have done all that I promised you," God said.

Joseph, husband to Mary, the mother of Jesus, similarly was given important messages by angels in dreams, according to the book of Matthew. While betrothed to Mary, Joseph learned of her pregnancy, and resolved to divorce her quietly. Before he did so, an angel appeared to him in a dream and said, "Joseph, son of David, do not fear to take Mary your wife, for that which is conceived in her is of the Holy Spirit; she will bear a son, and you shall call his name Jesus, for he will save his people from their sins."

Joseph followed the angel's instructions. After Jesus was born, Joseph was again contacted by an angel in his dreams. The angel told him to take Mary and Jesus and flee Bethlehem, for King Herod was intent to search for the child and destroy him. Joseph took Mary and Jesus and fled to Egypt, where they remained until Herod was dead.

That angels appear in dreams is significant, for dreams have a reality of their own—they are just as real as our waking consciousness. In dreams, we leave the boundaries of the physical world behind and travel to higher, more subtle planes. These planes are more subjective, but the subjectivity does not render dreams any less "real."

This fundamental wisdom about the reality of dreams has been recognized since ancient times. The early Greeks and Romans believed that the soul traveled while the body was asleep. The soul would go to otherworldly realms wherein dwelled the lesser spirits who served as intermediaries between humans and the gods. Plato called this realm the *metaxu,* or "the between." Here the human soul had experiences and encounters that had the same validity as waking life experiences. What made the dream experiences more special, however, was their supernatural nature. In dreams, it was possible to meet the gods, see the distant past or future, and be healed of illness and disease.

The *metaxu* is where we commune with angels while asleep. They give us information or inspiration. They may appear as angels, or as mysterious beings, or disguised as human beings.

Dream literature provides numerous accounts of writers, poets, scientists, musicians, and inventors who were directly inspired by dreams. Many arrived at answers to questions and solutions to problems that eluded them in waking consciousness. Were they given those inspirations by angels, who used the fertile medium of the *metaxu* to plant ideas?

Physicist Neils Bohr saw the model for the atom in a dream, and the nineteenth-century Russian chemist Mendeleev had a dream vision of the periodic table of elements. Artist William Blake was shown a process for copper engraving in a dream; the inexpensive production technique then enabled him to make a living from his mystical illustrations. Author Robert Louis Stevenson received the idea for *The Strange Case of Dr Jekyll and Mr Hyde* in a dream, and poet William Coleridge wrote his fragment, *Kubla Khan,* word for word as he remembered from a dream. He might have completed his work had he not been interrupted while committing it to paper. When he returned to his task, he discovered, unhappily, that it had evaporated from memory. Dreams are fleeting—they must be recorded immediately upon awakening if we are to retain and benefit from their content.

The ancients believed that such inspirations were indeed gifts from the gods. Or, as we might think today, from angels.

Patricia P., of Harrison, New York, is a born-again Christian who feels in close communion with God, Jesus and angels. "I feel I have a lot of angels around me because that's what it says in the Bible—there are many of them around us," she told me. Angels, she said, helped her rescue her little niece from drowning one day. The experience began with a dream:

> One night several years ago, I was in my bed at home in a house with my brother and his wife. I felt led by the Word—an inner feeling that I believe is Jesus Christ—telling me to pray that there would be angels around the swimming pool outside. We have a small above-ground pool in the backyard. There are a lot of children in the neighborhood, including my niece and nephew, who go into the pool. So, I prayed as directed. I envisioned angels standing around the pool's ledge facing inward. They looked like Roman guards, ready for protection. I don't know why they had that appearance, that's just how they popped up. I didn't anticipate that there might be an accident. In fact, I kind of questioned why I had been directed to pray that.
>
> A day or two later, I found myself in the pool with the little children. I don't know why I got in—I usually don't use it. Mostly, it's for the kids. They splash around with floaters on their arms to keep them up. I was standing in the water at one edge, and a friend came over and started talking to me, diverting my attention.
>
> My sister was nearby but out of sight. She suddenly felt the Lord say to her, 'Check on Lisa,' her daughter who is two-and-a-half years old. She looked around and realized Lisa was not present. 'Patty, is Lisa in the pool?' she called out. I didn't hear her, and she called out again, 'Patty, is Lisa in the pool?' I heard her, and turned around just in time to see my little niece step off the ladder into the pool at the other end without her little floaters on. She sank immediately under water. 'Oh, My God!' I shouted, and I started running towards her in the water. But the water was heavy, and it seemed like I couldn't get to her in time. Then I heard an authoritative masculine voice, about a foot away from my right ear, say, 'Swim to her!' I felt a presence, as though someone were standing near to me.

I swam to Lisa, and I scooped her out of the water by her arms. Her eyes were open so wide they almost seemed to pop out of her head. By then my sister had reached the pool, and she took Lisa and began banging her on the back. Water spurted out of her mouth, and she coughed and began breathing again. She was all right!

I thank the Lord that her life was saved. Lisa didn't suffer any damage. Truly, it was a miracle.

Later, I asked the Lord whose voice I'd heard in the pool, that said, 'Swim to her!' It wasn't the voice of Jesus, because I know that voice. The answer was given to me that it was an angel. And I know it was."

Since then, Patricia said, she has called on angels many times whenever she feels in need of their protection or guidance.

Dreams were the initial medium of my own encounters with an angel I named Silver Lady. In the mid-1980s, I started to have periodic "unusual" dreams that were significantly different from my dreaming pattern. I usually dream in color, but these dreams were almost always in black-and-white. The setting was always an alien landscape, unlike anything I'd ever seen on earth. The landscapes often were bleak and barren, sometimes like deserts, sometimes like the moon. Sometimes, the setting was nothing but blackness, like the black void of space.

In these dreams, I was always in the company of a tall woman dressed in flowing garments of a luminescent silver—hence my name for her, Silver Lady. We never spoke, but communicated telepathically. Only once did I see her face. It had no features like a human countenance. Instead, it was a swirl of iridescent color, like mother-of-pearl.

Silver Lady always took me somewhere for the purpose of instruction, though when I awoke, I could never remember exactly what it was that I had been told. I had some ideas from the imageries. For example, I was shown other worlds where realities were unlike that of the earth. I was taken into space and shown how to make a path of light for myself, by projection of thought. It seemed that I was being introduced to the multidimensional nature of consciousness, and to the tremendous power of thought. I was getting lessons in how we create our reality with our thought: we can either live in our own fear and darkness, or we can light our own way, and the way for others.

The dreams with Silver Lady became more frequent. They were wonderful and adventuresome, and I missed them if a period of time went by without one. I assumed her to be an angel.

Then something spectacular happened—I had an encounter. Encounters with nonphysical and nonhuman beings often follow a pattern. They often take place in the middle of the night. The percipient is often paralyzed. There is telepathic communication that infuses the percipient with information. There may be paranormal phenomena, such as levitation or the psychokinetic (mind over matter) movement of objects.

I awakened at about 3 AM to find Silver Lady standing beside the bed. She looked real and solid, though she glowed with a shimmery silver light. She was holding her arms outstretched, as though she were going to bend down and touch me, but we never made physical contact. Instead, a stream of energy poured through her hands, entering me between and slightly above the brows, where the third eye chakra is located, and in the chest, where the heart chakra resides.

This energy was a data stream. Bits of information were coming into me at a tremendous speed. I felt as though I were being downloaded by a cosmic computer. Information or knowledge was pouring into me so fast that I could not discern what it was. It was all I could do to absorb it, and I didn't feel I could do that without literally exploding. Yet, I was powerless to shut it off, for I was paralyzed and held flat to the bed by an invisible force.

The infusion seemed to last forever, though the entire episode probably was over in a matter of moments. At some point, I felt I could no longer absorb it, and the connection ended. Silver Lady vanished. I felt disoriented, got up for a few moments, and then returned to bed and fell immediately asleep.

The experience had a profound effect on me. I hadn't been shaken or scared by it, but wasn't certain what had taken place. My interpretation is that I had been infused with a blueprint of my work in this life. Furthermore, if I adhered to my vision of my path in life and trusted in my intuition and spiritual guidance, and applied myself with diligence, then doors would open before me according to this blueprint, or plan. And so it has been ever since.

With the infusion, a major role for Silver Lady was completed. It would be years before she appeared again, in a session with the noted

English medium and healer, Eddie Burks, which I describe later on in the book. Yet, I feel her guiding presence is always with me.

### Visions, apparitions and voices

A mystical vision is one of the most dramatic ways an angel can manifest. Unlike the mysterious stranger, who has the appearance of a flesh-and-blood human being, angels in mystical visions are bathed in a glory of light and radiate supreme joy and love. The percipient is overwhelmed by the light and love, and is in awe of being in proximity to God through his emissaries, the angels. Such visions usually have an instructional purpose, and a tremendous transformative effect on the person.

Many spiritual leaders have received their initiation by way of an angelic mystical vision. Enoch's visions were described earlier. Other Biblical figures, when they were called by God to be prophets, experienced mystical visions of heaven and angels. For example, Isaiah, who lived in the late eighth century BC, was shown the throne of God, encircled by seraphim.

Muhammad (c. 570 or 571-632), the founder of Islam, received the revelations of the Qur'an in a series of angelic visions. In 610, Muhammad was 40 years old and living a life of asceticism when, one night in his dreams, the archangel Gabriel appeared and gave him the first revelation of the Qur'an, the holy book that contains the doctrine of Islam. Muslims call this event the "Night of Power." For the rest of his life, Muhammad fell into nearly daily trances, during which he received the remainder of the Qur'an, which totals 6,666 verses. Sometimes the material was delivered by angels, and sometimes via clairaudient voices. Muhammad's trances were heavy and his breath was labored. Three years after his first vision, Muhammad began his new calling as a prophet, preaching first to members of his own clan.

Joseph Smith, Jr. (1805-1844), the founder of Mormonism (the Church of Jesus Christ of Latter-day Saints), had various visions, including of angels and pillars of light, that contributed to persecution against him. On the night of September 21, 1823, he was awakened by a brilliant light flooding his room. The light revealed the angel Moroni, a messenger from God. Moroni told Smith that he had helped write, then bury, a history written on gold plates by his father, Mormon, of an ancient people descended from Israel who had lived and died in America. Moroni said that Christ had appeared to these people after his resurrection, and that they had established a church, but that knowledge of the gospel was lost in a great fratricidal war. God had chosen Smith to retrieve the plates, translate them, and reestablish the church in preparation for the latter days prior to the Second Coming.

Moroni appeared to Smith three times during that night, and again the next day. He revealed the hiding place of the gold plates, but instructed Smith to wait four years before digging them up. Smith did as ordered, and retrieved the plates on September 22, 1827. He also recovered seer stones, the Urim and Thummim, and their breastplate.

The plates were covered with strange symbols resembling hieroglyphics. They created quite a stir among the public. To avoid harassment, Smith left western New York where he was living and went to Pennsylvania. He translated the symbols with the help of an itinerant school teacher. The result, the Book of Mormon, was published in 1830. Moroni recovered the plates and the stones and took them away.

Teresa of Avila (1515-1582), Spanish mystic and Carmelite nun, began experiencing mystical visions and revelations in 1555. She evaluated her visions through several criteria, which still can be used today in evaluating encounters with angelic beings:

— The visions have a sense of power and authority.
— They produce tranquility and a desire to praise God.
— They impart an inner certainty that what is envisioned
  is true.
— They are clear and distinct, with each part carrying great
  meaning.
— They result in a life of improved ethics and increased
  psychological integration.

Emanuel Swedenborg (1688-1772) traveled often to heaven in his mystical flights. The Swedish scientist and scholar led a routine life until 1743, when he was 56 years old. The spiritual world was thrust upon him one night in a dream, during which he visited the higher planes. For the rest of his life, he experienced mystical dreams, visions and ecstatic trances, in which he communicated with angels (whom he considered to be the souls of the dead), Jesus, and God. He visited heaven and hell. He was shown the order of the universe, which was significantly different from the teachings of the Christian church. Swedenborg understood that he had been chosen by God to see these things, and record them to teach others.

Swedenborg quit his government job and lived on a half pension in order to devote his entire attention to his visions. Initially, he had to rely on their spontaneity. Eventually, he learned to induce trances through breath control. Some of his trances were so deep that he remained in them for up to three days, seeming to others to be barely alive. While in light trances, he recorded the dictations of angels.

The experiences stimulated a tremendous outpouring of written works, which led to the founding of a religion in his name, the Church of the New Jerusalem.

Some modern angel encounters involve visual apparitions. The most common forms are columns or pillars of light, or balls of light, which are intensely bright white, white-gold or silver. The percipient receives mental impressions that these light-forms are angels. I have seen angels in this manner. Their light was so intense that I could not look directly at it. I knew they were angels, and I also received mental impressions as to the purpose of their visit.

Sometimes people see figures or outlines of figures within the light, which usually are human-like in shape. People occasionally see large wings. It is not uncommon for the lower portions of the figure to fade off into nothingness, or for hands, feet and faces to be poorly defined or not defined at all.

Angels also can appear as visions on the inner planes via clairvoyance and can be heard via clairaudience, that is, seen with the inner eye. Rudolf Steiner (1861-1925), founder of Anthroposophy, had numerous experiences on higher planes through clairvoyance and clairaudience, as well as out-of-body travel. Anthroposophy is a unique blend of Rosicrucian, Theosophical and Christian traditions. Through deep and concentrated meditation, Steiner learned to access nonphysical realms, including the Akashic Records, the master records of everything that has ever occurred everywhere in the cosmos. The Akashic Records exist as impressions on the astral plane. Steiner learned a great deal about angels, which he described in detail in his writings and many lectures.

Like Pseudo-Dionysius, Steiner perceived nine orders of angels in a hierarchy around God. However, he gave the levels different names and descriptions than Pseudo-Dionysius. Steiner believed his own spiritual work was service to the archangel Michael, who, he said, is directing the evolution of the human spirit into the third millennium.

## Channeling

Research for this book led me to Roseann Cervelli, a channeler of angels in New Jersey. Like others who have been touched by angels, Roseann experienced spiritual growth and tremendous changes in her outlook on life and her approach to living. Some of her channelings have been published in a book, *Voices of Love.*

"I was raised Catholic and I've always had a strong sense of spirituality," Roseann told me. "In my twenties, I went through a period of questioning the Church, and I became increasingly unsatisfied with the way it dealt with issues and people because of outdated rules and regulations. I went through an agnostic searching. I studied with the Edgar Cayce material for a number of years. And I began studying about healing and consciousness, and the Christ consciousness.

"Around 1980, I received a laying on of hands from a priest, who later became my mentor. I experienced a feeling of peace, like an opening. After that, for the next year or so, I studied with the priest and other like-minded people. I would have a kind of mystical experience. I would be pulled into a oneness and meditative state, and it would be so wonderful that I would just find myself in tears, just in being one with everybody on the earth. I'd see a face, like the face of my daughter, and then her face became somebody else's face, which became somebody else's face, and so on, and before I knew it, I was like enveloped in this oneness. These were my first experiences with the spiritual energies—very loving and very embracing. I didn't understand at all what happening. I thought I was going crazy. But I trusted the experience, because it *was* happening to me."

The mystical experiences lasted for about a year and then subsided. By then, Roseann was able to easily enter meditative states on her own. At the end of 1981, she met a woman who channeled an entity named Matthew.

"Matthew spoke to me about healing and about how, if I wanted to be a healer, I had to learn to love myself. He told me to do a meditation each day where I would walk along a beach, and see myself lifted up on a cloud. There I would meet Jesus or a lighted entity, and would be taken to a library where I would just absorb knowledge. I didn't have to know what that was, but I just had to be there. Then I would come back down to earth and spread that knowledge around.

"I did that meditation for about a week when the writing started. I was in my house vacuuming my floors and being a regular old housewife, and all of a sudden I got this energy coming through my head. I heard the words, *'pick up your pen and write.'* It was such a loving energy, and such a driving energy at the same time, so that's what I did. The first words that came out are the first words in my book, *Voices of Love:* 'Words are the essence of God.'

"The writing lasted maybe five minutes. It was quite an experience, because the thoughts were coming faster than I could write them down. I was hearing them from a different part of my being. They weren't coming just from my head the way I would normally write—the thoughts were almost ahead of themselves. I wrote quickly and my hand was shaking, there was all this energy. Then it stopped as quickly as it started."

Excited, Roseann called her priest mentor, who said, "Praise God, this is a wonderful gift! Sit with it and see what happens."

She did, and a few minutes later, the channeling resumed, again for a few minutes. "I was in wonder at what was unfolding," Roseann said. After that, I would feel called to write almost at any time—during the middle of the night, two o'clock in the morning. I finally had to ask to receive three times a day, so that it wouldn't disrupt my life.

"What I was given were little essays on spiritual concepts, like forgiveness, belonging, oneness, healing, and the healing touch. They were all teaching me to live a healing life. Any time I said or did anything, I would be aware of the impact. I also saw how I could use any situation to bless other people and myself as well, because I was tuned in to the Source, and I would be channeling love from the Source. I got to understand about the soul. As I wrote, it transformed me. It was like there was a spirit in my head, and it would go into my heart and I would emotionally *feel* what I was writing, and I could feel it changing me as I wrote."

The beings who were the source of the channelings identified themselves as Matthew and Elliott. They described themselves as teachers, and that their work was in service to humanity.

After about a month of Matthew and Elliott, a new energy introduced itself by saying, "My name is John, and I have come to teach about self-love." The John energy alternated with Matthew and Elliott. Roseann could feel distinct differences among them.

She soon shared her meditation essays with a close friend, Noelle. Noelle liked them so much that she asked Roseann to channel for her. Soon a small group formed—Roseann, Noelle and her husband, and a few others. The group began meeting at Roseann's home to hear channelings and discuss the material. They were told by their spirit advisers that, on a higher level of consciousness, they had volunteered to come together and work to bring others into the light. A book would come out of their work.

"It was incredible," said Roseann. "But it all unfolded just as they said it would. The channeled writing for every session began to form a story, a step-by-step progression for developing the inner self."

After a while, Matthew, Elliott, and John announced that they would be leaving Roseann, and would be replaced by another energy. "They told us that this was an angelic energy, the angels of light, and the angels were going to instruct us on a higher vibration," Roseann said. "Around Easter, the first phase of the new energy came in for the first time. It was so loving—it was a love I'd never known on Earth. It was very, very vast. I cried while I was writing, just because I was so loved. They called me "dear one" or "beautiful one," and it was so exalting."

The new energy remained with Roseann for two to three years, and then another change occurred. "The energy introduced itself as the Angels of Light and Truthful Revelation. They said that they were going to help us to reveal who we truly are in our daily lives, to bring all these teachings to an earthly form so that we could truly see ourselves and reveal ourselves and not be afraid to be chosen of light."

"This was a collective energy without personal names?" I asked.

"Yes. When the group first started, everyone wanted to know their guardian angel's name. At one meeting, I channeled all these names—some I could barely pronounce. Later on as we grew, we were told that the name was like a key to tune into the angel energy, but that where the angels are, there is such a oneness that individuality is not necessary. The energy is us as well—we are part of the angels, we are one with them.

"Let me explain it another way. Matthew, Elliott, and John were like teachers giving the information, whereas the angel energy is more experiential and loftier. I use the image of the mountain: with Matthew,

Elliott, and John, we were on the lower part of the mountain, and with the angels, we were higher. It's an embracing energy that gives a sense of belonging. I believe that we're all one, anyway, and that we can, through love, be lifted up to a higher vibration, that which is who we truly are. The angels, in their lovingness of us, helped us to love ourselves. They gave us a mirror image of our unlimited selves."

"How have these experiences affected your life?" I asked.

"They changed everything," Roseann said. "I had never felt that I could be loved so deeply, and this realization that I could was a great gift. I changed the way I saw myself, and the way I saw other people. Where I used to be afraid to step into a room because I didn't know if I would be welcome, I know now that I am always welcome, that everything in that room is part of me, and everybody is a part of me.

"Another significant change was that I'm not judgmental anymore. There's just no way I can judge anybody, because in my eyes, everybody is loving. Now, I don't mean to sound that I'm in denial of earthly realities. I'm not. I'm an alcohol counselor on the earth plane. I see things clearly. But that's not the only reality, and what I've learned is to speak in my heart. When I speak to others, I keep it in my heart that I am teaching to their Higher Self as well. There is a wisdom inside of each soul, a remembrance, and I feel that I'm here to help people remember that wisdom.

"These experiences made me belong to life," said Roseann. "I always used to feel separated, lonely, and lost, always needing to prove myself, or seek acceptance. Now I feel part of everything—part of the trees, part of the mountains, part of the people. Part of the best things that happen to me, and part of the worst things that happen. They're *all* part of me. By constantly loving it all, it gets transformed into love, which is a reflection of God."

Roseann said that some members of her immediate family were not able to understand the changes that had unfolded in her life, or the channelings. The breakup of her marriage also seemed to be part of her transformation, occurring at the time when Matthew, Elliott, and John were making their entrance. Matthew told her, "It is now your time to become a universal spirit, a universal soul. You have many to reach, and being with Peter is not where your life's path is anymore. You love him and he loves you, but it's time to separate."

"Even to this day, when people ask us why we got divorced, we say we don't really know," said Roseann. "It's strange. There was never hostility. We just grew in different directions and had different things to do, though those things weren't manifested at that time. It was just the way it was supposed to be.

"I could never have done all this if we had stayed married. I wouldn't have had the lessons about being on my own and learning how to grow up and do all the things that I had always been so dependent on other people to do for me. I had to learn to rely on not only invisible help through the angels and guides, but on the visible manifestation of that help. If you work hard enough on the invisible, it's got to manifest physically. It may take a little while, because it's much harder to change a physical reality than it is to change a thought. Physical changes start with thoughts, however."

The key to manifestation, said Roseann, is "loving everything" in your life, everything that happens to you. Embracing it all and accepting it as part of your life experience. Then you can move on. "Trust whatever difficulty is manifesting," she said. "It's there for a reason, and the angels have helped us to accept everything as a friend. There are no enemies. If we think that an experience is our enemy, we're going to miss the boat, and it's going to become a greater enemy. But once you love it, it gets comforted. The angel teachings we've received help you to accept and integrate everything that happens to them. You have breathed these things into life! Nobody else did, you did! You can change things by the essence of your breath, which is your vital force. If you breathe anger, you will create angry situations. But if you breathe love—truly the breath of life—you create loving situations. The angels teach us that you are the conduit for the life force called God, and how you breathe it in and out will reflect in your reality."

I asked Roseann to describe the process by which she receives messages from the angels.

"It feels different, depending on whether I speak it or write it," she said. "When I speak it, I'm speaking and hearing at the same time, so it's like I become the words. It is one dance. I hear and feel everything I'm saying, even though I never know what I'm going to say. When I write it, it goes a little deeper into me, perhaps because I hear it in silence in my head.

"You see, if we separate ourselves from angels or from a voice of love, we're also separating ourselves from God. And we are not separate from God. We *are* God, sparks of God, so we are sparks of angels, we are sparks of each other. So we are one. We'll never get to know God as long as we think he's outside of us. Not only is God inside of us, but he *is* us. There are people who feel that angels and God are outside of them, and then there are those who think that angels and God are inside of them. And then there's the next step, those who know that they and the angels and God are one. I have had the moments of knowing that oneness."

"That must be exquisite," I said.

"It's bliss. You are yourself and everything else at the same time. Being everything, you know your individuality more. It's a strange experience.

"I've had two of these experiences. One was a dream. In the dream, I was in a hospital room, lying on a table. There were doctors with masks on. They were going to take a picture of me. When they went to shoot the camera, all of a sudden I experienced myself as a mass of loving energy. This was me, this was the picture. I was in such bliss that I was crying in the dream, and I woke up from it crying, because of the joy I felt. I was me and I was everything, and I was just massive energy. It was beautiful and special."

The second experience occurred when Roseann, Noelle and Noelle's husband were in Maine hiking through forests down the backside of a mountain. Suddenly all three of them slipped into an expanded, timeless moment in which they felt themselves a part of the trees and everything around them. The experience altered Roseann's conscious point of view. "Trees have never been the same for me," she said. "Trees are me now, wherever I go."

Roseann said that one of the "high signs" that the angels gave her and her group was the number 22. In numerology, 22 is a master number, of high vibration. Their awareness of this secret sign of sorts came about through a series of synchronicities involving 22 and combinations of two's, such as $2.22 and 2:22 o'clock. When such numbers pop up spontaneously, they are taken as a sign that the angels are communicating their ongoing presence. For example, once Noelle wandered through a grocery store in a low state of mind, muttering to herself, "I am weary unto death, I am weary unto death." When she reached the checkout stand, her purchases totaled $2.22. It was a signal to her to snap out of her mood.

Once Roseann was to give a presentation to teachers, and was assigned room number 222. She smiled to herself. The angels had the last laugh, for she discovered that there was no room 222. There was a 220 and a 221, but no 222. She was told it was a typing error, but Roseann felt there had been no mistake. The angels had given her the high sign to let her know that she was doing what she was supposed to be doing in life—a sort of "you're on the right track, and we're with you!"

It is interesting that the angels working with Jayne Howard Feldman selected August 22 as the date for Be An Angel Day. Jayne and Roseann had never met.

### Death and near-death apparitions

Angels stand by us throughout life. When our time comes to leave the earth plane, they assist us across the threshold to the next world.

The appearance of angels, spirits of the dead or other spirit helpers at the time of death has been recorded throughout history. People who are conscious right before death sometimes exclaim on the sudden presence of a radiant deceased loved one, an angel, or another religious figure, such as Jesus or the Virgin Mary. Psychical researchers call such figures "deathbed apparitions" or "take-away apparitions."

Around the turn of the twentieth century, psychical researchers began collecting anecdotal accounts of these figures. Most notable is the work done by William Barrett, an English professor of physics and one of the most famous early psychical researchers. Barrett became interested in deathbed apparitions because his wife was a doctor, and she heard numerous accounts of them in her work. He published a book on the subject, *Death-Bed Visions: The Psychical Experiences of the Dying,* in 1926.

Several decades later, two other researchers, Karlis Osis and Erlendur Haraldsson, both well-known in parapsychology, added considerable material to the subject with the publication of their book, *At the Hour of Death.* Osis and Haraldsson examined tens of thousands of reports of deathbed apparitions collected in the United States and India.

Skeptics contend that such visions are due to lack of oxygen, hallucinations, drugs, disease or depersonalization. Yet, none of these possible explanations satisfactorily explains the visions. Furthermore, the visions are seen by the dying who are not heavily sedated or delirious, but who are fully conscious.

Occasionally, others can see the take-away angels as well. Shirley C., of Phoenix, Arizona, told me a story passed down to her by her mother, Louise, about Shirley's grandmother, Mary Louise:

> After all her children were grown [nine girls and four boys], all in good health, my grandmother became gravely ill and was taken to the hospital. The doctors told my grandfather that his wife was gravely ill and was going to die, so they put her in what was called the death room. Her sons would hear of no such thing, so the four of them went against the wishes of her doctor, went into the hospital, and carried her out, bed and all.
>
> When they got home, the girls nursed her back to health. Her hair had even turned white from the illness. When she was well again, her hair came in black as it was when she was young and healthy.
>
> She was very ill again at age 66, and all the children were notified to come home to see their mother for the last time. They were all there in the room with her, when a band of angels surrounded her bed. Her soul left her body and the angels disappeared.

Perhaps all the children were blessed with witnessing the angels because they had been so close to, and caring for, their mother.

Similarly, persons who have near-death experiences (NDEs), in which they have clinical death and then return to life, often report the same luminous figures. Some describe traveling down a tunnel toward a bright light accompanied by beings of light, or radiant spirits of the dead. When they reach a threshold, they may be told by these figures of light, or by voices they ascribe to angels, that they must return to earthly life. Sometimes they are offered a choice: to return or to pass the point of no return to the Other Side.

Joy Snell, a former English nurse, saw take-away apparitions frequently in her work in hospitals. She never told anyone what she saw, lest they think she was crazy. After her retirement, she wrote about her experiences in a moving book, *The Ministry of Angels*. Sometimes Snell saw angels arrive at the bedside of someone who was on the brink of death, and stand by ready for the moment of transition. Immediately upon death, the soul left the body and coalesced into a spirit body just above the corpse. It had the same radiance as that of the angels. Once the spirit body had formed, the angels took it away. Snell longed to visit the place where they went, but was told by a disembodied, authoritative voice that she could not, for her work on earth was not finished. The true Other Side is not to be glimpsed by the living.

Snell also saw other apparitions in the course of her work. One was a ministering angel who took the form of a middle-aged female nurse. At first, Snell thought this angel was a human. Snell would see this figure moving about wards only at night, touching sleeping or unconscious patients who had been in great pain and distress. The following morning, these patients reported that their pain was lessened or gone, or that they had experienced a profoundly restful night of sleep. Some said they'd had dreams in which they heard the most heavenly music. When Snell inquired who this fabulous nurse was, she discovered that no one on night duty matched the description.

Two others apparitions Snell saw were harbingers of death and life. The Angel of Death was a dark, shadowy, veiled figure that appeared at the foot of a patient's bed. No matter what the doctors said about the patient's chance for recovery, if the Angel of Death appeared, the patient always died within two to three days. Conversely, the Angel of Renewed Life forecast recovery. This angel appeared at the head of a patient's bed. He was a bright figure in a cloud-like, luminous robe, with a youthful, happy face. He always stood with his right arm raised and index figure pointing up, like a high sign. Again, no matter what the doctors said about the patient's chances of recovery—no matter how bleak—if the Angel of Renewed Life manifested, the patient always recovered.

Angels make themselves known to us in whatever manner and form are the best in order to reach any one individual. If we are receptive and open-minded, we become aware of angels moving among us all the time.

# 6

# Give Me A Sign

Angels can intervene dramatically in our lives to save us from certain tragedy. Angels also can give us important information that not only can change the course of our lives, but the lives of others as well. Most often, angels work in more gentle and subtle ways, guiding us in our thoughts and deeds on a daily basis. These personal interventions can have just as profound an effect on our beliefs and life philosophy as angel rescues. Such contact with angels can open us spiritually, steer us onto another course, or reaffirm that we're on the right track.

Here are personal accounts that demonstrate different ways angels aid us.

## "What should I do?"

Leslie of McLean, Virginia, faced a crossroads in life at age twenty-three. She turned to God for help, and her guardian angel stepped in:

> I was at a very low point in my life. A relationship that
> I had thought would be permanent was ending, I hated

my job, I didn't like my living arrangements, and a general dissatisfaction with my life was causing great despair. One cold November Sunday night I went to church. The auditorium was very large, seating between 1,000 and 2,000 people. On this night, attendance was sparse, and I sat on next to the last row with no one nearby. Waiting for the service to begin, I remember thinking to myself, 'God, what am I going to do?' A clearly audible voice said, 'Go back to school.' The voice was so clear I turned around to see who sat behind me. To my surprise, there was no one there.

I had never considered returning to school as a possible response to my situation, but the advice made such good sense that I quit my job, stored my furniture, and within three months was back in college as a full time student. The fact that I had only $700 to my name never seemed like an impediment, and of course, it wasn't. I was able to get loans and find jobs and assistantships all the way through my master's degree. Sometimes the work came in ways that were truly miraculous. My guardian angel seemed to be working overtime.

The truly amazing aspect of this experience was that I did not think it unusual or strange in any way. I never told anyone of the experience until years later, after I had become involved in a spiritual search. Only then did I truly recognize how I had been blessed, and I was amazed that I had the good sense to follow the guidance. I am very happy that I listened and acted.

In a similar at-a-crossroads situation, an angel manifested visibly to Phyllis M. of Santa Fe, New Mexico, and her young son. The experience is unusual, in that the apparition appeared to both of them at about the same time, but while each was in separate locations. Said Phyllis:

In 1984, I decided, very precipitously and most uncharacteristically for me, to take advantage of a new house I could rent in Santa Fe. Overnight, I made a plan to take a self-proclaimed 'sabbatical' and run away from New York City with my then eleven-year-old son. As we approached the departure date, I was racked with anxiety about the wisdom of my decision and how it would affect my young son being at such a distance from my ex-husband and my son's friends.

One night, close to the date to leave, I tossed and turned all night. At 4 AM I decided to get up to do some yoga exercises to try to relax, because I had a very full agenda for the next day. I was in a shoulder stand when I realized than an angel was suspended mid-air in my living room. My perception was that it was feminine and she was glowing in a light of luminescent white-gold. Although I did not 'hear' as one normally hears, I heard the message, 'Do not be afraid, you and your son are being led.' Then she was gone.

I rushed to my meditation seat in the hopes of trying to reconnect with this angel. I glanced at the living room clock. It was 4:45 AM. I was not even settled into my seat when I heard my son's footsteps. I was stunned because he *never* awoke during the course of the night. As he approached me, he said, 'Mom, I just had an apparition.' I said I had had one also, and asked him to tell me what happened. He said that there was a figure in his room, and while he could not see all the features clearly, he thought it was a woman. He then tried to describe luminescence, by saying she was surrounded in a strange light and that she had her arm outstretched and was pointing her finger. He indicated that he 'heard,' though it wasn't a voice he could describe, her say, 'Go!'

I asked him to show me which way her arm was stretched towards. It was west.

## Sealed with the Holy Spirit

If ever anyone needed an angelic high sign, it was Edith P. of Swannanoa, North Carolina. Edith, a devout Christian, had been struggling for years to cope with serious family problems. She described her experience:

Have you ever heard of the statement, 'Being born of food that has been much tried by fire'?" Well, in a spiritual sense, it means a person such as I, who has had to go through an awful lot of tragedies and negative situations in life, and in spite of it all, still desiring to become the person the Lord wants them to be.

As a child, I came from a broken home, with a family history filled with self-destructive people through suicides, alcoholism and murder. In going through all these negative experiences, with the family members bent on destroying themselves and those others around them, I realized that the only true 'parent' I could depend upon was God the Father Almighty. Even though I did feel like an orphan, having to be in and out of a children's home quite often due to family tragedies, I always knew that even though I felt like there was no one else there for me, there was always God.

Being unfamiliar with the many guises of alcoholism, I ended up marrying an alcoholic in 1968. My then-husband was a constant beer drinker, but it never dawned on me that the problems in our relationship were due to the fact that he was an alcoholic. As you can well imagine, I was living through a hellish situation, with his playing all sorts of psychological and emotional warfare to keep a wall between us. Until I came upon Al Anon, I truly believed that the problems were due to me. That was not the case at all, even though my alcoholic husband tried his hardest to make me look like the bad guy all the time.

In spite of all I was going through, I was very close to God. With my own mother committing suicide over my errant father, I kept praying to God to help make me the person he wanted me to be, in spite of everything. I told God that I did not want to commit suicide like my mother did to escape her situation from my father. I prayed constantly to God to *please help me*, even going into the closet and pouring my heart out to him with tears just streaming down my face.

Then one summer night, it happened! A new bedroom and bathroom addition had just been completed on our home, and my first daughter was at the other end of the house in the old bedroom. With her being just eighteen months old and still apt to wake up and cry during the night, I naturally wanted to be able to hear her cries. So, I purchased a plug-in intercom system. One was in her room, set permanently on the 'talk' position, and mine was set next to my side of the bed on the table, permanently set on the 'listen' position. This worked quite well, for the intercom also put out a faint light that served as a night light for me when I had to get up in the middle of the night to attend to her.

One June night, my husband and I had gone to bed. I was pregnant with my second daughter, who was due in December. I had closed my eyes but had not yet gone to sleep. Suddenly, I heard a voice doing mumbling or chanting of some sort. I immediately opened my eyes, because I thought it was my eighteen-month-old daughter starting to wake up and cry, and I would have to attend to her.

I was lying on my back and I did not expect to see what I saw! Above me, there appeared to be someone who looked female floating above me. She was chanting something in a language I had never heard, and all the while was moving her right hand across my forehead. I looked to the right side of my bed, and standing there was what appeared to be someone male. He was wearing a white robe. I quickly looked him up and down. There were long sleeves on his robe, and at the end of each sleeve were two bands of gold trim.

My eyes kept moving from the being above me to the one beside my bed. The standing one had his hands folded in front of him, his right hand over his left. He appeared to be dark-haired with dark eyes. He had such a wonderful expression on his face, as though he knew something I did not at the time. No words were spoken. I thought to myself, 'Are you from outer space?' In just a few minutes, the whole episode was over. The shock of what happened got me out of bed to go think about it.

After that, I read some books on angels and consulted with some Christian clergymen, trying to find out what the experience signified. With the spiritual insight I had after the experience, I knew that the Lord had sent those angels as a visible sign to me to let me know that he was sealing me with his Holy Spirit, and the angel above me was writing the Lord's name upon my forehead. I belonged to Him! And, he wanted me to be a witness to the sealing of his Holy Spirit upon me as an assurance to me, because he must have known that I needed that assurance. The clergymen weren't able to help me. They were only able to tell me that there are angels that God sends to aid those whom are to receive salvation.

## Minding morals

Bob is a retired officer of the U.S. Air Force. He grew up an Episcopalian, and throughout most of his life never gave much thought to angels, though he did feel uncommonly protected and lucky. While on a trip for the Air Force to Addis Ababa, Ethiopia, he had the first of several experiences that changed his mind about angels, and had other, far-reaching effects as well.

I was staying in a hotel, and I went to my room. There was a knock on the door, and suddenly there was one of the most beautiful women I've ever seen in my life standing there, very seductively. She had long blond hair and looked like the actress Barbara Eden. I was startled—she was so beautiful. I'd seen her around the hotel and had had some conversations with her. She invited me in her room. I was married-and still am—but I was torn, and was tempted to go. I declined her offer and she left. I wondered, did I make the right choice? Even though I love my wife, at the same time I was certainly tempted. My room had a Bible in it, and I started reading it, and thinking about that aspect of life.

When I got back home to the States a couple of days later, I was still thinking about all this as I drove home from the base. I hope this doesn't sound silly, but I was questioning, is there a God, and are there angels. As I was driving along, I said, 'God, if you're real, give me a sign!' No sooner had I said the words than a brilliant light came right at the windshield almost into the car. It was like a flash of lightning or a flashbulb going off right in front of me. I was so startled that I almost couldn't believe that it happened. I thought maybe I imagined the whole thing.

At home, I was greeted by my wife and kids, and I assured myself that I'd done the right thing back in Addis Ababa. I know it may sound obvious to you, but I grew up in a *Playboy* atmosphere where taking advantage of such a situation was considered the thing to do.

When I went to sleep that night, I was visited by a figure that I can only describe as an angel. I don't know whether I dreamed it, or I awoke and saw it in the bedroom. It was a shining white figure, a huge, tall man in robes, a very loving figure, just radiating love. He walked to the side of my bed and put his hand on me. He didn't say anything, but I got the impression that he was telling me that I had done a good job—the right thing.

When he touched my arm, I could feel a lot of love and warmth, and a feeling that he loved me. After I received this message, the figure just disappeared. It was certainly a religious experience! And it was real—as real as anything else in my life.

I was more convinced than ever that there is a God and that his guardian angels do exist. Afterward, I started reading about angels to find out more about them. I felt more of a connection to religion and had more interest in attending church. I became much closer to God. I was stimulated to study about other religions. I decided I was most comfortable with Christianity, but I could see the parallels among the different religions. Another thing that happened to me was that I became much more aware of the earth. I became active as an environmentalist in my town.

I definitely believe that God has a plan for us. In fact, there are some indications that the angels are in control. I don't necessarily mean that they decide every little thing that happens to us, but they're here in large numbers, and guarding us. What they decide is how the world goes. Conversely, there are the fallen angels who are trying to make bad things happen. They control some people, too. Various religions have the apocryphal story that there will be a great battle between good and evil.

I feel this angel is still around me. I feel that in time of trouble I can call on him. It gives me a lot of peace.

## It's the right thing to do

Jayne Howard Feldman is often given guidance by angels that she does not fully understand at the time. However, she long ago learned to trust the guidance, and so she follows it when it is given. Time and time again, what the angels say bears out. Sometimes, what she is guided to do has a great impact on another person, which Jayne herself could not have foreseen, as in the following experience:

I received a jewelry catalog in the mail, and in that catalog I saw a pair of simulated diamond earrings in the shape of dear little angels. I heard my guardian angel tell me that I should buy these earrings. I questioned that message, even though these were truly precious, because I had a pair of diamond studs. I could not fathom that I would ever wear these earrings in the catalog. However, I heard loud and clear that I was to buy them, and so I did.

The earrings arrived and sat in their little gift box on my dresser for about a month. Then one day I received a phone call from a close friend in New York. This wonderful woman had just returned from the doctor's office, where she had been told that she had cancer of the uterus. She was so frightened by the bleak prognosis. And she was very confused about decisions she had to make, and she knew she had to make them quickly. She asked if I would pray for her, and I told her I would begin immediately.

When I hung up the phone and got up from my chair, I felt myself encircled by the most loving angels of service, who were chiming to me in unison that I needed to package up the earrings—they were for this woman to wear. They were to be sent to her immediately as a gift from the angels with this message: when she wore them, the angels would be there whispering in her ears, 'We love you. It's going to be all right. Don't be frightened. We are here with you. You are not alone.' The angels added that I was to tell this woman that she was to wear these earrings in 'good health,' because that was what the angels were sending her—blessings of good health. And so I followed those instructions and the earrings were on their way to New York.

Several days later, I received a call from my friend. She stated that the earrings had arrived on a day when she was having a battery of exams and tests, and they were truly a gift of strength from heaven. My friend commented that this had been one of the lowest days in her life until the angelic gift of love arrived. She felt the earrings were truly a miracle. She has since shared with me the inspiration that the earrings have given her to face the challenges at this time. The angels constantly reassure her by the presence of the 'angelic present' that she is not alone, and to open herself to the gifts of heaven, which include healing—and sometimes even a pair of earrings.

# 7

# The Otherworld Contacts of Eddie Burks

While researching in England, I shared remarkable experiences of angels and devas with a wonderful medium, Eddie Burks. I was referred to Eddie by the College for Psychic Studies in London, and we became close friends. Eddie had contact with the dead, angels, and other spirits. He aided earthbound souls, investigated hauntings, and performed spiritual healing. How Eddie developed and used his talent is quite a story. His path is an example of how the spiritual life unfolds for many people, and how our experiences lead us through one door to another. If we follow the light that shines ahead of us, even if we are not certain where it will lead, great transformation takes place.

When I met Eddie, he was living and working at Inlight House, a small retreat center near the elegant village of Grayshott in Surrey. The setting was fairytale—a tidy brick country house with a fresh appearance, set on lovely, landscaped private grounds next to a government-owned forest trust. Eddie had instilled a soothing energy throughout the house. At night, especially when the moon rode high in the sky, the woods and lawn were full of dancing fairies and nature spirits. It was a magical place, and it was there that Eddie connected me to angels and also devas in a way I had never before experienced.

For two days, I was a guest at Inlight House, and I literally inhaled the spiritual energy of the place. Eddie and I had many conversations, some with cups of tea before a cozy fire in the drawing room, and some on pleasant and long walks on the grounds and into town.

### An early awakening

Eddie's first peek into the world of spirits came at an early age. "I had a near-death experience at the age of five or six, coming out of an operation for a tonsillectomy," he told me. "This was in London—I was born in the East End (a working class area). During this near-death experience, I went somewhere wonderful—I just can't tell you how wonderful that was. Coming back, I felt myself hurtling along a tunnel. I was very, very upset, angry even, that I'd been taken away from somewhere that was so wonderful that I couldn't bear to leave it. This tunnel experience haunted me for years. I dreamed about it about once a month until the age of thirty. It was more of a nightmare, because I was so angry at having been torn away from this place. Disappointed like a little child would be. When I was thirty, I read about the tunnel experience for the first time, and was able to put the experience into context and realize what it was all about. And I never dreamt about it anymore after that, because I'd now dealt with it."

"Did that experience influence your later psychic awareness?" I asked.

"Oh, yes," Eddie agreed. "It actually set me on the road, got me searching. But the effect it had immediately on me was that I realized in Sunday School that they were not telling us the truth. They were teaching us about New Testament, but they never told us what I had experienced. They were missing this great big piece that was so important. This is what I wanted to know more about, and I couldn't find it in the church.

"So I started to look for the truth as soon as I was old enough to be able to do that. I read philosophy at the ages of eleven and twelve, thinking that I would find this truth that I knew was there but I couldn't reach. I discovered that philosophy was barren as far as that search was concerned. Then one day, while still roaming through the library books in the local library, I came across a book called *Encyclopedia of Psychic Science,* with a foreword by Sir Oliver Lodge, and I knew I was home. I got interested through that in the Spiritualist movement, and that was an interest that came and went. I was in the army four-and-a-half years, and then after the war [World War II] there was a period where I wasn't active in the spiritual field because I was bringing up a family and making a career as a civil engineer."

### First visits from the dead

Eddie continued, "It wasn't until 1970, when my first wife died unexpectedly at age fifty-one and then came back to me posthumously a number of times that my awareness began to show itself. In 1981, my only son and only child by my first marriage, dropped dead in the same way as had my wife, with a burst aorta artery. He was thirty-five. The events around that left me no doubt about survival after death. It was a repeat of what had happened with my wife, but stronger."

"How did your wife and son come back?" I asked.

"Margaret—we called her Peggy—came back the day after she died. My son had come back to the house from Derby, which was about twenty-five miles from where I was living, to be with me. We were both feeling utterly miserable. Lunchtime came and I said we must eat something. So I took out of the refrigerator a chicken which I had shared with my wife the day before, and there was some of it left over. My son was standing near me, and I was morosely cutting up this chicken, and suddenly I burst out laughing. My son thought that I'd flipped. I said, 'It's all right, it's all right, Michael. Your mother is here and she is reminding me about what happened yesterday.' And she was. She was reminding me that I'd cut chicken up the day before, put all the good bits on her plate, scruffy bits on mine, and the two plates somehow got interchanged, and I had all the good stuff and she had all the poor bits. We laughed about it at the time. She was using this event to lift me out of my sadness, you see. From that point on, I felt so different. I was walking on air. She kept coming back and I knew she was around. I knew she had survived. I couldn't see her, but I got a lot of information telepathically from her. That went on quite some time.

"At the time he died, Michael was living in Scotland, where he had gone to get a job. He was living with a girl that he was hoping to marry, his first marriage having broken up. When the lady concerned phoned me to let me know that he died, I went straight up by train. The following morning I went out to get a death certificate. When I went back into the house, she was busy at the kitchen sink. And as I walked into the room, it was as though I had walked into Michael. I said to her, 'Good heavens, Michael's here.' She didn't even turn round. She said, 'I know he is. I've been talking to him.' She's psychic, too, but she had repressed it for a number of years. Her psychism was resurrected by his death. Michael was with us a number of times in the days that followed. When I returned five days later to my home in Nottinghamshire, I again felt his presence and continued to feel his presence on and off for quite a time, then less frequently as time passed. But I was never thinking that I was bringing him back. He was coming back out of sheer love, I think, because we were very close."

Peggy's presence also diminished over time—both she and her son were evolving in their own right on the Other Side. "Three or four months after my wife died, I went to Blakely on the Norfolk coast for a weekend merely to relive the memories of a holiday we had a fortnight before she died. I was rather disappointed because I was unaware of her over that weekend. I felt sure she would make an appearance, but she didn't. So I got in the car to come back. It's a three-hour journey. As soon as I sat in the car, she was in the passenger's seat at the side of me. We held a mental conversation for an hour-and-a-half. At the end of it she said, 'I have to go now, and you won't be hearing from me for some time.' In an instant she'd gone. I didn't hear from her for a long while. I feel sure that during that period, she went through the self-judgment. When she next contacted me, I could feel there was a difference—she was more etherealized somehow. She's come back at widely-spaced intervals since."

### Called into healing service

"At the end of 1984 to early 1985, I was suddenly pitched into healing work. It was spontaneous. As I developed the healing, doors opened in my awareness, and I would find myself involved in other aspects of the person's life.

"For about six years before this, I'd been aware of a presence with me, and it would come to me at any time. I might be driving, I might be watching television, I might be reading, I might be at my office desk. It was benign, and I knew it could be trusted. It brought me a great feeling of uplift and peace.

"I could sense it, but I couldn't hear it or see it. I could sense it, sense it very strongly. It was nearly always on my right side, somewhere behind me. Quite close up, almost like a cloud hovering there."

The first indication that the spirit had arrived to help Eddie become a healer happened spontaneously. "One day I went to see a friend whose wife had just come out of hospital after having a severe spinal operation," he said. "I went on the spur of the moment. Five minutes before I got there, she got out of bed for the first time since she returned from hospital, put her dressing gown on, and sat in the living room, as though she were expecting me. I tried to start a conversation with her, but I realized she was too weak. So, I started to talk past her, towards her husband. She suddenly intervened and said, 'Have you brought a spiritual presence into the room?' The moment I acknowledged it, I simply had to get up and take her hands, and *whoosh!* something happened. A surge of wonderful power or energy just flowed straight through me towards her. I'd never had this happen before."

"What was your reaction?" I asked.

"Amazement, absolute amazement. It was as though a switch was thrown. A fortnight later, at the age of nearly 70, she was dancing on the patio in the back garden to show me how quickly she'd recovered. She was going out shopping. She lived for another seven or eight years. From that day on, I've been coming across people that I have to help."

One person Eddie helped was a woman who was diagnosed with uterine cancer. He gave her healing prior to her entering the hospital for radiation treatment and a hysterectomy. During the healing, he saw a light shining at the end of a tunnel, and was told that he wasn't to say anything about it.

Eddie visited the woman several days after the operation. She was sitting up beaming. "The sister is amazed at the way I've come through it," she told Eddie. "But we know why, don't we?"

"Yes, we do," Eddie responded.

"I've still got to learn the results of the tests they've done to find out whether I have any malignant cells floating about me," she said.

"You'll find it is clear," Eddie said, thinking of the light at the end of the tunnel.

Sure enough, no malignancy was detected. After several months, the woman was well enough to return to work. She learned to drive a car for the first time, and embarked on a life full of activity.

As time went on, Eddie experienced an increasing inner urge to help people with healing. People would come to his house after work, as many as seven in an evening. Eddie did a laying on of hands, following his intuition. Eventually, the healing work expanded to include the release of earthbound souls.

### Angels and spirit guides come forward

Eddie received direction from nonphysical beings, sometimes without knowing who they were. "I'm sure there is an angelic presence, and I always invoke an angelic presence," he said. "I ask in a silent blessing that I give at the end of each healing for the angelic being most linked with that person to be able to draw close and give guidance and help in whatever way is necessary. I'm much less specific in my healing now, because I've come to realize, as most healers do after a time, that we don't know enough to be specific about how the healing should be applied. Some people need their illness, for example, and it's not up to us to intervene to take that illness away. It's really part of their karmic past, and they must deal with it. So I try to make my healing non-specific, and hand over to whatever presence is with me, including the angelic presence that I always feel is close."

Eddie said that he sensed a Native American presence with him. "The reason why so many people working in this field think they have Indian guides or helpers is because this is the one race that we most need for their experience at this time," he said.

### Accessing the higher planes

I asked Eddie to describe his process of tuning in to higher dimensions.

"I suppose the nearest description I can give is that I allow no force, but I allow my consciousness to respond to a different level," he said. "It's a tuning, and sometimes it has to be a fairly fine tuning. I am aware sometimes of tuning into much higher levels than others. It's as though my consciousness goes into a lift or an elevator. In some subtle way the elevator goes up taking my conscious with it, and knows the level at which it has to stop. How on earth it does it, I don't know. But I'm more and more conscious of the immense powers of the mind and the fact that we are only just touching on the edge of it. I don't try to do this—using will power wouldn't do any good. Trying it out of curiosity wouldn't work either. It seems to be the result of a purposeful desire to do something for others.

"I remember looking for a man, a suicide. In an instant the feeling I had was that some part of my mind was sweeping round, almost like a searchlight. Within seconds it located this man. How it really did it, I don't know—I only get an impression. Someone who has passed over recently is much easier to find than someone who went on, say, a couple of years ago. They are at much different levels.

"If I go too far, I feel as though an elastic band inside my brain on my right side is being stretched. It's a physical discomfort, a warning sign, and I know that I mustn't go beyond that. That is the nearest physical effect I get. Something else worth mentioning: if I'm approached by an entity that is good, then the approach seems to be made from the right-hand side. On the rare occasions I'm approached by an entity that's evil—and most of them, fortunately, don't seem to be able to break through my defenses— then they come on the left side. So, for me, the left is the bad, the right is good. When I'm moving up in consciousness, I'm moving into a brighter light. And light and spiritual heights are synonymous, the same way that evil and darkness are synonymous. Not synonymous, but they almost interchange. But light and love, darkness and hatred, seem to behold to each other, very clearly."

Eddie said he often received clairvoyant impressions when he worked with earthbound souls, some of whom had been stuck for centuries. "I often see the costume they're wearing, which gives me a very good idea of what period of history they belong to," he said. "This impression is often confirmed in other ways. I see them after I've been through the initial stages of catharsis [the death process] with them. I see someone, or an animal, come to escort them away."

"An animal?"

"It's an animal with which that person is familiar—a pet, a favorite horse, for example. I once released a man who had been trapped [earthbound] since the end of the eighteenth century, and after I'd been through the catharsis of his death and the things that entrapped him, and he released those emotional energies that were holding him down, I was wondering how he would get away. A large black horse came onto the scene, and he recognized it. It was a horse he loved. He mounted that horse, and the horse trotted out to the courtyard where this scene took place. I was told the horse knows the pastures to which the man belongs."

**Earthbounds and spirit releasement**

I asked Eddie to tell me how he became involved in spirit releasement work, and what the process is like.

"One of the first events that led me in that direction occurred in the early 1980s when I was at the College of Psychic Studies, and I was talking to Brenda Marshall, the president, in her office. I said to her that suddenly I was aware that I'd got someone with me who seemed to be deformed. I could feel this man's presence. There was a lot of noise going on outside with pneumatic drills being used close by. The first thing this man said to me was, 'London always was a noisy place, wasn't it?' That was his introduction. I could tell that this man was seriously deformed—it was having an effect on me. You would perhaps call the condition spastic nowadays. It was clear, also, that he was stuck, trapped in the earth plane. I also got this distinct feeling that there was something wrong. And so I tuned further into him, and he was saying to me, 'I don't want to go where he is, I don't want to go where he is.' He was talking about the cruel master that he had when he was on earth. He was a servant in the Victorian period. This other man had treated him abominably. In fact, the servant said to me that the only relief he got was when he was beaten, as though his life was so terrible that this was an event that somehow put some relief into him. He was afraid that when he died, he would meet up again with this man. He was so terrified that he fixed himself—he wouldn't let himself move. I had to reassure him that he wouldn't find this man. Once he was reassured, and we'd been through the catharsis of death and the fear that was holding him, these binding energies were released. Somebody came and took him away into the light. Wonderful that was, that experience of being released into the light."

I asked Eddie what he meant by the "catharsis of death."

"The mechanics of the process, as I've come to understand them, are these: that the person being held down by some obsessive aspect of the mind, is trapped and can be trapped for a very long period. The first thing one has to do in releasing them is to go through those events which have relevance to this entrapment. Very often it's associated with the death itself. So, that means that one has to go through the death with them. I experience the way in which they died. I experience some of the pains that they went through, and I experience also some of the emotional problems that caused them to be stuck. It seems to me that it's rather like the process that people go through under psychiatry, where in order to relieve a neurosis the person is taken back to some event and then taken through the emotions of that event. Once those emotions are released there's subsequently the possibility of cure. It happens much more rapidly with these trapped souls—perhaps five, ten minutes or so before a presence comes onto the scene. This presence may be a relative or friend, and it may occasionally be an animal. There has to be a love connection. That person or animal then escorts the trapped individual onto a pathway which is flooded with light, and takes them to the spiritual levels where they should have gone in the first place had they not been trapped."

"Why does the process have to involve a living person such as yourself?" I asked.

"I know I work with a team on the Other Side who cooperate," Eddie said. "They in some way guide the trapped person into my orbit. They then go through the process I've described. That release of energy can be so great that it can cause the soul who is releasing it to, if you like, rebound into psychic space somewhere. My function is anchor man. I hold a soul steady until that release is effected. The team then come into play with the bringing of some person into the scene that the trapped soul recognizes, and has confidence in and will accompany. It is team effort, but this business of being anchor man is very, very important. Without it they on the other side would have very much more difficulty rescuing trapped souls."

"Could you explain more about this rebounding?"

"It's difficult to translate it into physical analogy. The impression I get is that when the person releases all this emotional energy that is tied up entrapment, it's like the recoil from a gun. They'll go out of the psychic space that they're in and be more difficult to find. We, being immersed in this material world, are in a good position to prevent that from happening, because we are less easily moved. The power of emotion at this level doesn't have the same effect as it does at the spirit level, where emotion has great power. It is largely a mental realm, and it is ideoplastic—it's a world in which thought can influence action in a very direct way. The release of emotional energy somehow causes the displacement of the person in what corresponds to space to us, but in whatever terms that may be in the next life."

"Why do people become stuck?" I asked.

"The reasons are many indeed. I keep coming across different ones. Perhaps one interesting reason concerned some of the people who died in the earthquake disaster in Armenia several years ago. I became aware that I was contacting people in connection with a disaster, and I wasn't sure what disaster it was. And then I saw the rubble of an earthquake disaster, and I knew: Armenia. I saw a man shepherding a number of people, trying to hold them together, because they were in a state of near panic. I gathered that these people hadn't realized that they'd died, and they were terrified that they would get caught up in another aftershock. They'd taken over with them their terror, and this was the thing that was trapping them. This man seemed to be a natural leader, and he was trying to keep them together.

"I found myself, or part of myself, standing on top of the rubble looking down on them. I tried to project calm and quiet, but I hadn't any idea how this was going to develop. It's difficult to say how many people there were—perhaps twenty or thirty. It went through my mind that they were going to be very difficult to release from this situation because of their near panic. I thought, 'If some angelic figure comes onto the scene or somebody very bright, there's going to be no holding them.'

"Then an amazing thing happened. I saw a flock of sheep moving onto the scene, towards these people. In Armenia sheep are an everyday thing. But one of the sheep moved towards one of the men, and gently nudged him, and somehow got the man to understand that he should follow him. The man followed the sheep, then the next sheep went to the next person, and so it went on until they'd all been led away. The sheep were leading them, you see, to an area where they would be away from all this rubble and where they would be at peace. They would move on from there to a proper release. But I didn't need to follow it any further. That was it."

"How do you anchor the trapped soul and prevent them from ricocheting into psychic space?"

"I do it mentally—I'm working on a mental level. The mind is so powerful. I was once told, after releasing somebody who'd been trapped for hundreds of years, to observe the power of the mind—how at one extreme it can pin a soul down in time and space, and on the other extreme it can encompass the universe. That just about sums it up. If the mind, which is so powerful in a post-mortal condition, if the mind has some obsessive idea, which may be terror or greed, or is fixed on the notion that there is no such thing as survival, then the mind makes sure that the soul is fixed. Won't let it move. I could tell you innumerable stories of this sort of thing. I've got in excess of 150 cases. They're all different, which makes them very interesting."

"Do you have any idea how many souls are trapped?" I wondered.

"It's a small minority of people, that's for sure, but it is still a significant number. The chances of one getting trapped, I would guess, is less than one in several hundred. But the entrapment can persist for a long time. I have come across cases where people have been trapped for hundreds of years."

"Do any earthbound souls attach themselves to living people and cause problems?"

"Sometimes, but usually not," Eddie said. "I've recently come across one or two cases where mothers have been possessively attached to their daughters. That can cause a lot of unpleasantness, and it's a big relief to the daughter once the mother is escorted away. But it's not a forced release— none of it is forced. The soul concerned has to begin to understand that they're in the wrong place. Once they understand that, they can move on.

"One of the most remarkable cases I've come across like that was at the College of Psychic Studies where I happened to be one day. I don't go there very often. The president, Brenda Marshall, asked me to see a lady who'd just come in, with a pain in her head or neck. She'd been carrying this pain around for the last seven years, and she'd been in countries all over the world seeking relief. She'd also been on morphine, but nothing did anything for it. So I met the lady, and we went into one of the rooms, and I started to talk to her and tune into her. I became aware that there was a presence with her. I described this presence, and she recognized it as a man, a Mexican whom she'd nursed through terminal cancer. He died of a tumor on the brain. This presence became very strong, and then I made contact with him. I went through his death experience with him, and released him from entrapment. It seemed that as the tumor developed he went into a coma. He was forced out of his body and saw it lying on the bed. He could neither get in it nor get away from it, because the body was still alive. He became very, very frustrated. When he died, he attached himself to this lady, because, as he said to me, when he went away from her he went into a darkness. In this attachment he was transferring to her the still very vivid memory of all the pain that he went through, and she was experiencing his pain. He apologized for having caused her this pain. Then it was possible to get help for him. The team on the other side, whoever they are, took him away. Her pain went immediately. I realized her aura or etheric body was damaged because of his attachment. I worked for some time, about twenty minutes, doing my best to seal her aura off. I walked out and left her to sit quietly on her own. A few minutes later she came out, rushing round the college saying, 'He's done a miracle, he's done a miracle!'

"I had another case involving a lady who felt uneasy about her mother, who had passed over," Eddie went on. "I quickly found the mother, and I saw a room that looked like a kitchen. In front of the fireplace there was a trap door. Just as I came onto the scene, somebody had gone down through the trap door and was about to slam the door down. It was the mother. Didn't want me to find her. I said to the daughter, 'It's no good me trying to pursue her down there. She doesn't want to be found, and I can't find her if she doesn't want to be found. We'll have to leave her for a bit and hope that something can be done in the meantime.'

"I came back to the scene the next day. This time I was able to make contact with the mother. She had been watching her daughter's actions, or as much as she could perceive of them through a little window in the kitchen wall. This window, I could see, was about eight inches wide by about fourteen tall. It looked like smoked glass. Whenever she wanted to make contact with her daughter, which was most of the time, she would be peering through this little window. It reminded me of what St. Paul felt, 'seen through a glass darkly.'

"This illustrates something that I've found time and time again that at this other, post-mortem level—what we would regard as allegorical becomes real. It's important, I think, that I keep coming across this. The mother was seeing her daughter through this allegorical window, but it was a real window to her. Through this she was interfering a lot with her daughter. She was influencing her and her mind would be reaching out towards her daughter, trying to control her. It was a very nasty situation.

"When I found the mother, I had to persuade her to step into a circle of light that had appeared before her. It took some time to persuade her to do this. She stood and eventually she made the step. Once she stepped into it, the background of the kitchen faded away. That was no longer relevant. I suppose it was a change of vibration. She was escorted away, and I knew she'd got a journey to make. In a case where somebody has been causing mischief, they don't go straight to the spirit world at the level that most people enter. They have a journey to make, and it's an upward journey that has many allegorical aspects in it. They find obstructions, and they've got to get past them— they can't dodge them. Each one represents some psychological or moral aspect of what they've got to overcome on this journey. They're invariably escorted, sometime invisibly, sometimes visibly by somebody, and sometimes even by an animal.

"A beloved animal again?"

"This whole business of the part played by animals is intriguing," Eddie said. "I've found animals playing all sorts of roles. Love is always a part of it. I came across a man who had committed suicide, and who was trapped as a result. People tend go into limbo when they commit suicide, and they don't get released. It's reckoned that as a rule they don't get released until the end of what would have been their natural life. They don't appreciate the passage of time while they're in that condition. Unfortunately, whatever problems caused them to commit suicide tend to keep recycling for them all the time. They don't get away from them. It's a terrible, terrible existence. However, if people commit suicide under circumstances where they haven't the responsibility for their actions, it's a way different story.

"When I found this man trapped by suicide, I discovered something important—that we can intercede, that our prayerful thoughts for them can result in an amelioration of their condition. That's why it's so important to pray for those who committed suicide and to send them love. It's very precious to them in their condition, very precious.

"This man was feeling his loneliness. It was a terrible loneliness. I asked for help for him. A little dog appeared. I knew that little dog would stay with him through the period of entrapment. To that man, it was a great help.

"I also came across a man who had committed suicide by gassing himself with exhaust in the back of a small van. I was asked to look into this on behalf of his family, who wanted to know where he was and what had happened to him after death. When I picked him up he was lying in a small box on his elbow, propped up in the attitude that he was in when he died. I couldn't make out what this small box was. It was only later I discovered that he had gassed himself in the back of a small van, and that's what I was seeing. His mental picture of where he was, was the same. The thought of him being stuck there many years, until his life would have expired naturally was so awful. I asked if something could be done for him. After a time he was lifted out of this van in a most remarkable way. He was just levitated out of this van in the light, and he was put into a little grotto. Now, he was still confined, and he wouldn't be able to move outside that little grotto, but it was a tremendous improvement on where he had been. This is the sort of thing we can do to help. I don't think we need to be psychic to do this. I think if we know somebody who has committed suicide, and we ask that their lot be ameliorated as much as possible, then these sort of things will happen."

Eddie had another case that illustrated the impact of mortal emotions on the post-mortem state. "I suddenly became aware of contact with a woman, and that she was in great distress. I tuned in and I began to see her. She was dressed in Victorian costume. I got the impression of the late nineteenth century. She was wheeling a market barrow.

"She started to say, 'I cared for them, I looked after them, and they didn't bother with me when I grew old.' I gathered that she was terribly upset because she'd brought up quite a large family, and worked very hard in the market with her husband. When her husband died she still carried on. She brought the children up. When they were grown up, she felt they didn't help her enough. She was having to go on working in the market with this heavy barrow, taking the goods there, and selling them and wheeling it back again in order to earn enough money to keep herself alive. She became embittered about this. Understandable, in a way.

"This was what had trapped her, so I went through all this with her. Still, she seemed to have something that hadn't revealed itself. Then it began to show. I could see her standing in this cobbled street—this was the cobbled street of her memory, if you like. It was her mental construct that she was in. She said, 'God shouldn't have let it happen, God shouldn't have let it happen.' She began to rail against God. She grew more and more angry as she released this. Then she started to run. She ran along this cobbled road and tripped over her own skirts, fell headlong. She was beating the ground with her fists as she lay there, and shouting and in a terrible state of distress, and so very angry with God. Once she'd finished expressing all this anger, she got up, and after a time she was escorted away into the light.

"I could see that what had entrapped her was her feelings of deep religious guilt that she was blaming God for her situation. She couldn't come face to face with that. She felt unworthy because she was blaming God. She was a very difficult thing. When she was escorted away, I thought to myself, that's good, she's gone. A voice said to me, 'What are you going to do about the anger?' I puzzled about this.

"Then I saw what appeared to be a globe of glass or plastic, or a bubble, huge, about three or four feet across, poised three or four feet above the ground where this cobbled road was. Inside it were flames and a great deal of activity. A very menacing looking thing. 'What are you going to do about that?' the voice asked. I said, 'What can I do about it?' The voice said, 'You've got to dissolve it with love.'

"I projected love around this object as it was hovering. Gradually it got smaller and smaller and smaller until it vanished. Then I was told, 'If you'd not done this, this would have drifted about and then caused a great deal of harm if it had touched someone either at the earth level or the next level.'"

## The Angel of Operations

Eddie had a glimpse of an angel in one healing. "I started to do healing with the lady who'd learned she'd got cancer, and had the hysterectomy. When I went to see her, while I was talking to her, I realized that there would be an angelic presence with her when she went in for this operation. I asked her to visualize this, and to try and draw it closer to her. This I did on other occasions with people who were going in for operations involving general anesthetic. I felt there was always an angelic presence going with them. Once saw this angelic presence, but not fully. I saw the edge of a garment, and it was a brilliant white. And I knew that I wasn't seeing the whole of this figure, because it would have been too blinding. I came to progressively understand how important it was for people, if they could, to understand that an angel was present. I think the reason for the angel being present, particularly in operations where there is a general anesthetic, is that the operation is like a near death. The soul is moved out of the body and therefore has to be protected so that nothing else can gain entry. Just as there is an angel present at death, so this angel is present during operations. I used to call this the Angel of Operations. I couldn't think of any other word for it.

"I made a point when I knew somebody was going to have an operation of always invoking this angel. It would always be there, but I think if the person undergoing the operation could be made to understand that it was there, then the presence could be drawn closer and a lot of help would come out of it. This has been people's experience—in a number of cases they've felt that there was a presence with them."

### Guardian angels

I asked Eddie for his thoughts on guardian angels.

"I think angels are present in other circumstance of importance," he said. "For example, at birth. I'm sure that they play a major part in that process, and in the process of conception right up to birth. I believe that there is a hierarchy of angels just as there is a hierarchy of most spirit entities. There is a level in the angelic kingdom where angels overlook houses. I sometimes wonder, if a house becomes empty, that the reason why it falls into decay is as much because the angel withdraws as that it is due to physical decay. A house that's been empty for a long time has a great sadness about it. It's got something lacking. We think the thing it's lacking is, it's got nobody living in it. But I think it goes beyond that. The house has ceased to function in the way that a life has function."

### Angels incarnating as humans

Eddie went on, "I've had one stunning experience in relation to angels. This was a case where an angelic being elected to come into the human race. It happens rarely. A lady I knew several years ago was very concerned about her grandson. He was a highly intelligent boy. She is psychic and was aware that he was in touch with the darker psychic side on the astral level. Yet, surprisingly, he seemed to be in control. This was very puzzling. In fact, in terms of normal human experience, he was taking awful risks, and he was virtually playing games with certain entities on that level. He also seemed to be getting himself into all sorts of mischief, including scrapes with the police. He was behaving in such a way that she was concerned he'd end up in prison. One night I woke up and I was told that this young man, who was about sixteen, was an angelic being who'd elected to come back into the human race. In doing this, he brought with him some remembrance of his former powers at an unconscious level. It was this remembrance that was leading him into the sort of adventures he was having with the dark side, in which he seemed, surprisingly, to be able to control events. I was also told that at a deeper level he was anxious to get as much experience as fast as possible in the human situation. This was leading him into the sort of behavior that we would regard as very chancy.

"I told the grandmother that I thought it was possible that he would go on getting himself into trouble. That he might even foreshorten his life through an accident of some such, in order to come back after a fairly short interval to learn more in different circumstances. It was as though this being that was projecting as this boy, had a need to learn as much as possible as quickly as possible. When we looked at his behavior in the light of this, and what she already knew about him, it did account for the things that were puzzling her, and she accepted this. It helped her in one way that she could see that there was a reason and a logic behind the way he was behaving.

"What happened to him?" I asked.

"He continued to get himself into trouble, and the last time I heard about him, he was up for several court cases."

"Why would an angel elect to come into the human race?"

"I think the angelic kingdom is trusted with much power because it's incorruptible," Eddie answered. "This is why God uses the angels as his messengers. The same power could not be given to human beings because they couldn't be trusted with it. They are so corruptible. The angelic kingdom watches the human kingdom, and is very—it's difficult to find quite the right word—is very interested, almost envious—of the way that the human race can advance spiritually through suffering. The angelic kingdom is unable to do this. It doesn't find itself in these sorts of situations that the human kingdom does."

"How do angels advance then?"

"They have to advance through service. The reason why an angel occasionally elects to come into the human race is that this particular entity is willing to sacrifice its peculiar advantages as an angel in order to advance virtually in the same way that the human being can advance. It is possible that such a being will connect to and revert back into the angelic kingdom at some point in the distant future."

"Does that mean that angels have souls?"

"The angels are eternal beings. They show themselves ordinarily in a form that we can recognize, but, in fact, they are creatures beyond body.

They show themselves in ways that we imagine they should look like. Much the same as the fairy kingdom shows itself in ways that we can recognize. But they are, at least the higher levels, far beyond the need for form."

### The roles of angels and devas

I asked Eddie, "Do you think angels are assigned roles or functions?"

"There are angels with all sorts of functions," Eddie answered. "There are angels who are concerned with landscape and with looking after people and guarding homes, or at least overlighting homes in a spiritual sense. There are angels who have a degree of spiritual responsibility towards nations, and others who have a degree of responsibility towards the clearest aspects of the planet earth. These functions are, to some degree, in parallel with those of the devic kingdom. The devic kingdom is in a relationship to the angelic kingdom that is like the relationship we have with the angelic and devic kingdoms. They are parallel, cooperating beings, and all are progressing upwards."

"Toward what?" I asked.

"Toward God, toward greater wisdom and understanding of God's ultimate purpose. We know that we are, in this life and in the many lives that we have, gathering together experience both of good and evil, and that we are taking this experience with us and joining into groups, and that we garner out of this experience the aspects which will carry us forward to higher and higher levels. We start as pure and innocent spirits and have to fall, as Adam and Eve fell, and then work our way steadily upwards. In the process we've lost the innocence, but we've gathered wisdom."

"If angels can advance through service, why would they want to do it through suffering?"

"Suffering brings about a different sort and faster rate of development," Eddie responded.

"Do you have any idea how many angels might be walking among us for various reasons?"

"No. I've learned more and more not to discount anything. I was once told that we set limits on our capabilities and our understandings through our imagination. If only we were to set free our imagination in a constructive way, we could advance more in the spiritual and psychic realms. Always around us, in the mental field, there is a horizon which we ourselves set. We push it back every now and again, but we would make faster progress in some directions if we were to free our imagination in a constructive way."

"Why is it important for human beings to become closer to the angel realm, and how is it possible?"

"First of all, it is God's purpose that we do cooperate with the angelic kingdom. I think that the angelic kingdom has been waiting a very long time for the opportunity for us to recognize their existence. The angelic kingdom has fallen out of recognition with most people in the Western world, who relegate the whole idea to the Old Testament and the stories there, and think that angel stories don't happen anymore. We think that the angelic kingdom, if it ever existed, served their purpose with God in the Old Testament times. In this way, the angelic kingdom has had to stand aside for most people, sadly waiting for human beings to come round to the realization that many of the problems that have beset us, and particularly those that beset us now in regard to the planet, can only be solved by recognizing their existence and cooperating with them. They have the power, the understanding to help us in ways that we are powerless to work. It's absolutely vital that we recognize this."

"And how can we reach out to them?"

"By transferring the notion of the angelic kingdom at mind or intellectual level down to the heart level, so it becomes a deep conviction. We must work on that conviction. The more the imagination opens constructively to recognize that there is this possibility, then the closer we shall become to angels and the faster we shall be able to transfer what is an intellectual understanding at best into this deeper heartfelt conviction. When we reach that heart level, then cooperation can become real, and we shall begin to have an inner knowing and an inner understanding of the angelic purpose. After all, the power they harness could be used—and should be used—in solving our problems."

Eddie continued, "Angels have a special relationship between us and the devic kingdom. The devic kingdom has a somewhat narrower horizon, with duties of or relating to all natural events, and all those things which are necessary to try and put the earth to rights. But the angelic kingdom has access to powers of a different sort to that of the devic kingdom. The devic kingdom has immense powers that would dwarf anything that man has ever been able to achieve in the way of power. Of that I am certain, because I've had some contact with that. The angelic kingdom has a different quality of power, a more spiritual power. The spiritual power is somehow mediated, so that it can be used in cooperation with the devic power. Here again, the human race has a vital part to play. Then we shall begin to reverse the sort of harm that we've done to the earth."

"How have you experienced the devic kingdom?"

"A number of times I've had the devic approach made to me by devas of the air, devas that control wind and storm and so on. The feeling that they give is not the same as the feeling one gets from spiritual entities, or human spiritual entities. It is a degree of detachment. There is the feeling that the devic kingdom, in following the pathway of action that is set for it, is quite prepared to wreak destruction at the human level. It doesn't want to, but it is prepared to do so if that is what is necessary. The devic kingdom stands aside to some degree. It does offer us cooperation, it does ask us to respect it. But if we don't, then it's quite capable of bringing about such forces that can cause great damage.

"If we continue to damage the earth, we should bring about the results that are being caused by our action. In manifesting these results, the devic kingdom would be immediately affected. They wouldn't react in any vengeful way. They have indicated that they are capable of withdrawing their cooperation in matters like crop growth, and if we continue to break the spiritual laws that we should be obeying, they might do so. Again, it's not revenge, it's simply that they would have to withdraw cooperation because cooperation with us would be impossible."

"Do devas take forms the same way angels take forms?" I asked.

"I've never seen a deva. But they seem to be able, without any difficulty at all, to communicate intelligently to us, and invariably bring with them a certain degree of detachment, and also an immense, awesome power, especially those that relate to the physical kingdom as distinct from the plant kingdom. This awesome power is very restrained. Quite clearly their primary interest is not us at all. Their primary interest is in making the physical kingdom and the plant kingdom and the rest of nature operate as it's supposed to operate.

"What we've got to do is to recognize that there are these three kingdoms and probably others. The human spiritual kingdom, angelic kingdom and the devic kingdom have all got their part to play, and in their various functioning they all need each other."

I wondered if animals have angels that look over them.

"They certainly have devic protectors," Eddie said. "Each species has a devic spirit which guards it, guides it and is responsible for its future development."

Eddie said that he did not believe that the angelic kingdom directly intervenes at the physical level. Instead, they bring powers to bear which both the human and devic kingdoms can use.

## Eddie channels the angels

After spending two fascinating days with Eddie learning about his work, I asked him if he could contact the angel realm for me. "I'd like to ask them for their advice concerning my research," I said.

Eddie agreed, though he pointed out that he had never before attempted to directly contact the angel realm, primarily because of the intensity of the energy there. He was uncertain that his human consciousness could access such brilliance, but he would give it a try. The session turned out to be one of the most incredible I've ever experienced with a medium.

We got comfortable in the sitting room at Inlight House. The room had been warmed with heaters and a fire, and Eddie turned the heat down. I sat on the chintz sofa, notebook and pen ready to take down dictation. Eddie sat opposite me on a straight-backed chair.

Eddie closed his eyes and began the process of elevating his consciousness. I closed my eyes and relaxed, soaking up the pleasant atmosphere that saturated the house.

After some time—I was not sure how many minutes had passed—I was suddenly aware of a presence in the room. I opened my eyes but could see nothing out of the ordinary. Yet a presence was there, so powerful and intense that it created a pressure in the room, as though we were plunged under water. I had the feeling that the presence was light that was beyond the ability of the human eye to perceive. In addition, I felt the room become hot, even though the heat was turned down.

The pressure and heat built in intensity. Then Eddie, eyes closed, began to speak. I was able to focus on what he was saying, and write it down. The session lasted but a few minutes, and the pressure continued to build until it became almost painful. Yet, it was a pleasant pain, if that makes any sense. I can only compare it to the ecstatic pain experienced by some mystics.

The message delivered was this:

> Your interest in the angelic kingdom is purposeful, the full import of which will only be revealed in the course of time. You are being used by the angelic kingdom as a willing and valuable servant to help bring about a greater awareness of the angelic function. Be prepared at some stage to be lifted in your inner vision. What you see will tax your powers of description. This will be presented to you by those angels working most closely with you. You are not yet ready for this illumination.
>
> We call upon you to tune into this kingdom not by act of will but by dedication likened to sanctified purpose. Our kingdom is one of great light, and few humans are fit to view it. You will be given the necessary protection.
>
> As for your work, rest assured that we take sufficient measure according to our purpose. Remember this also: do not reduce us in any way to suit humanity's understanding. This would not be right. Raise humanity instead to meet us through inspired understanding. Impress on people that we are not as they. We are not human. We are no closer to God than you are. But we serve his purpose in a way that you would judge to be more direct. We express a power that you would not understand as yet, except if you experience it. The word you would choose would be 'ineffable.'
>
> We differ from you in a number of essential ways. We have no pride. But we have much love. We bear the very essence of unconditional love. Yet, we have the power to direct this and place it where God would have us do so. We seek earnestly to raise the human understanding, to bring it to a sufficient level where the answers to pressing problems can be found. We shall not give the answers—that is not our function. These will come from the devic kingdom working closely with those inspired in the human kingdom.

So, do you see our function more clearly? In your writing, check what you say against what has been given here, and you will do us a great service, and in turn, humanity. Our blessings come to you now, shafted in intense light, which would not be fitting for you to see, but which will lift you and inspire you in the work ahead. We say farewell with the thought that you and we are likewise children of God doing his purpose.

As the message was finished, the pressure in the room began to dissipate. I didn't want the presence to leave. "Don't go!" I thought, but the presence continued to withdraw. I asked if I could pose questions. The angels responded through Eddie, "Yes."

For a few moments, I was stymied, torn between personal matters and cosmic matters. As if they read my thoughts, the angels admonished, "Do not trivialize."

I decided to ask what had puzzled me for years. "Who is Silver Lady?"

There was a moment of silence, and then Silver Lady herself came on the scene to answer. "You do not have quite an accurate picture of me," she said. "I am not an angel, but am of the angel realm and of the human realm. My function is to be intermediate between the angel kingdom and the human kingdom for the purpose of interpretation. Seek not to identify me more closely at this stage."

And with that, Eddie could no longer physically sustain his effort, and the connection was broken.

After a session, Eddie does a visualization to close down his chakras. But the intensity of the angel kingdom was so great that he found himself unable to shut down his psychic centers himself. He was in obvious discomfort, shaky, red in the face, with trickles of sweat running down his cheeks. He directed me to place his hands over his shoulder blades. I did so, and felt like I'd placed my hands inches over a radiator. Heat was pouring from his body. I made smoothing motions in his aura, which he said would help his pituitary gland. After several minutes he felt all right.

We discussed the session. Eddie said that as he had begun his meditation to send his consciousness to the angel realm, he had felt a being—some sort of helping spirit—come between him and the angels.

This measure was protective, intended to buffer the intense angelic energy, which otherwise would have overwhelmed Eddie's consciousness. The being remained in place throughout the reading. I thought that some sort of buffer had protected me as well, making me aware of light that was beyond my ability to see it, without destroying my senses.

I was particularly struck by the angels' statement that they are no closer to God than are humans, but just tread a different path. That contradicts what has been handed down to us by philosophers and church authorities. Yet, it made sense to me.

As for Silver Lady, we were both surprised at her description of herself, which indicated that she might be half human, half angel—a sort of hybrid we'd never before contemplated. We wondered how many other hybrids there might be, and where they existed in relation to the angel realm. I also was puzzled why I'd been admonished not to inquire more into her identity or nature. I wanted immediately to have the uplifting the angels described. However, nearly two years would elapse before that occurred.

Since then, when I've described the session to others, I've been asked why the angels did not define themselves in terms of "What is an angel?" In fact, they did, by describing their function and nature. Angels are beyond definition in the human sense, and we waste a lot of time looking at trees and missing the forest. Instead of being preoccupied with what angels "are" and look like, we should focus on their essence: unconditional love.

### Eddie channels the devas

The session with the angels was wonderful enough, but it was my last night in England on this particular trip, and so Eddie graciously agreed to contact the deva realm as well. I was curious to see what they might say about crop circles, those mysterious formations impressed by unknown means into grain crops in England and elsewhere in the world. I had been researching them, looking for causes and purposes.

First, we relaxed and regained our energy by going for a long walk in the beautiful woods around Inlight House. It was late fall, and most of the trees were bare. We then walked a trail into the village of Grayshott, where we had tea and cakes. After supper back at Inlight House, we returned to the sitting room for another session.

The deva session was much different than the angel session. As Eddie shifted his consciousness, the heat in the room rose, as it had during the angel session. And, as in the angel session, I felt an intensity, a pressure in the room, only of a much different sort. It was not light-beyond-human-ability-to-see. Instead, the energy welled up from the earth, and was outside the house as well as in it. I could feel it mostly as a pressure against my sinuses and chest. It was a primal energy, raw and hard, the energy of tempests and hurricanes and tornadoes. This energy was controlled by the devas who answered our call. I felt that this energy could easily be turned against us in a destructive way, if the devas were so inclined. The wind, which had been still throughout the day and early evening, began to blow harder and harder, and to whip around the house in an eerie scream.

To reach the devas, Eddie first made contact with the spirit of a Native American, who offered to perform the dance that would summon the beings we sought. As he danced, Eddie tapped out the rhythm with his hands. Then the message came:

> Those of my race knew of the devic kingdom. We could call them up when we needed special help. There was a special rhythm—a drum rhythm—and a dance for each one. For the spirit of the trees, for the spirit of the sky, and of the wind, and of the rain, and the rivers, and the plains, and the mountains. Our lives were intimately woven into the fabric of nature, and the supernatural beings who governed all these aspects.
>
> You wish to make contact with the devic kingdom. I will dance for you. And beat out the rhythm with my feet to call up my brother, the spirit of the land. He is one with whom you need to get better acquainted. It would help if you made the room quiet.

I got up and turned off the stereo, which was playing Gregorian chant. The wind came up outside. After I resumed my seat, there were a few moments of silence, and then Eddie spoke again, this time in a voice distinctly different from that of the Native American spirit:

When will you learn? We watch and wait. And feel the pain as you destroy our kingdom. Time is running out. The land you desecrate will lose its fertility. And the rain which is our friend shall wash away the soil, and the wind shall blow away the dust. And the dust shall settle on the upturned faces of those who would not learn.

This need not happen. But time is running out. We see encouraging signs here and here. A small awakening. But it must take hold.

You seek to tell of the reality of the angelic world. This is good. But you will make their task and ours and your own far more difficult unless you take heed. If it is a close run thing [pushing the limits of time], many will suffer and there will be despair. We can do certain things which lie within our power. But the many people that dwell on the earth must seek assistance from the source higher than themselves.

If the effort to do this manifests, we will be able to cooperate. We know already that humanity has a high price to pay for its foolishness. I am telling you what some are slowly coming to know. You must bend all your efforts in prayer to God to help you make the contacts that are essential if you are to turn the tide. We do the will of the Creator. We do not do man's will. In his ignorance he undoes much of our work. Why is he so blind?

It was a profound message, but did not address my question about crop circles. In fact, in both sessions, I did not necessarily get the information I sought. Instead, I got the information I needed, which is always the case when humanity turns to higher sources for help.

The messages that Eddie channeled stayed with me throughout the years. Every time I went to England, I always paid a visit to Eddie. After a couple of years, he left Inlight House and moved to Lincoln, where he continued his work. He taught me many things about contacting the spirit world and traveling around the astral plane.

# 8

# Healing Helpers

If angels make themselves available to help humankind, then surely one of their most important tasks is to heal. There are different kinds of healing—physical, emotional spiritual. When we are faced with catastrophic or terminal illness, or permanent injuries, sometimes we cannot be cured physically, but we can be healed spiritually. Many persons who work in medicine and health care have had strange experiences that are both wonderful and eerie, in which presences and energies from beyond the physical plane manifest to help the patient. In particular, persons who work in alternative healing are often acutely aware of presences that guide them in their work. Some call these presences God or Jesus; some call them angels.

The healing ministry of angels is established in Tobit, one of the books in the Catholic Bible, and also part of the apocryphal literature. Tobit tells how the angel Raphael, whose name means "the shining one who heals," provides magical formulae for healing. The story underscores the concept that angels do not act on their own, but are emissaries of God, and that they have no physical form, but can create the appearance of form for the benefit of humans.

The story is about a pious man named Tobit and his son, Tobias. It took place in the late eighth century BC in the Assyrian capital of Nineveh, where the people of Northern Israel had been taken captive. The storyteller is Tobit himself, who was instructed by Raphael to write an account of the events that happen to him, his son and others.

By his own description, Tobit was a model of piety, walking "in the ways of truth and righteousness." He gave money, food and clothing to the poor. He defied Sennacherib the king by burying his fellow Israeli dead, whose bodies were left in the open by their captors.

On one occasion, Tobit, who was fifty years old, was sitting down to dinner when he learned of another corpse that needed burying. He left his meal and attended to the body. He was defiled from handling the corpse and so did not return home that night, but slept by the wall of the courtyard. He left his face uncovered.

Unbeknownst to Tobit, sparrows were perched on the wall, and their droppings fell into his eyes, rendering him blind. He sought help of various physicians, to no avail. His wife was forced to work to earn money.

After eight years, Tobit, depressed and in despair, begged God to let him die. In preparation for death, he called in his only son and told him to journey to Media, where he had left some money in trust with another man. He instructed Tobias to find a man to accompany him on the journey, and he would pay the man's wages for his time and trouble.

While this drama was unfolding in Nineveh, another was taking place in Media. There, a young woman named Sarah was possessed by the demon Asmodeus, "the destroyer." Sarah had been given to seven men in wedlock in succession, but the demon had killed them all on their wedding nights, before the marriages could be consummated. Sarah's parents, Raguel and Edna, feared they would never marry off their only daughter.

God heard the prayers of both Tobit and Raguel, and dispatched Raphael to heal Tobit's blindness and exorcise the demons from Sarah.

When Tobias went looking for a man to accompany him on the trip to Media, he found Raphael, who appeared as a human and introduced himself as Azarius, the son of one of Tobit's relatives. They struck a deal for wages and departed.

The first evening, they camped along the Tigris River. Tobias went down to the river to wash, and a giant fish jumped up and threatened to swallow him. Raphael told him to catch it, which he did with his hands, and threw it up on the bank. Raphael said, "Cut open the fish and take the heart and liver and gall and put them away safely." Tobias did this. They then roasted and ate the rest of the fish.

Tobias asked the angel what use were the saved parts. Raphael replied, "As for the heart and the liver, if a demon or evil spirit gives trouble to any one, you make a smoke from these before the man or woman, and that person will never be troubled again. And as for the gall, anoint with it a man who has white films in his eyes, and he will be cured."

As they neared their destination, Raphael told Tobias that they would stay in the house of Raguel, and that he should take Sarah as his wife. Understandably, Tobias was not thrilled to learn that seven prospective husbands had all died at the hands of the demon. But the angel assured him, "When you enter the bridal chamber, you shall take live ashes of incense and lay upon them some of the heart and liver of the fish so as to make a smoke. Then the demon will smell it and flee away, and will never again return. And when you approach her, rise up, both of you, and cry out to the merciful God, and he will save you and have mercy on you. Do not be afraid, for she was destined for you from eternity. You will save her, and she will go with you, and I suppose you will have children by her."

The events came to pass as the angel predicted. Tobias was offered the hand of Sarah in marriage, and a contract was drawn up immediately. In the bridal chamber, Tobias followed Raphael's instructions for exorcising Asmodeus. The demon fled to "the remotest parts of Egypt" (the traditional home of magic and witchcraft), where Raphael bound him up.

After a fourteen-day wedding feast, Tobias, his bride and Raphael returned home to Tobit. Tobias anointed his father's eyes with the gall of the fish, and Tobit's sight was restored. In gratitude, he and Tobias offered Raphael half of the monies that Tobias had retrieved from Media.

The angel then revealed his true self to the men. "I am Raphael, one of the seven holy angels who present the prayers of the saints and enter in the presence of the glory of the Holy One," he said. He told Tobit that he had been ever present with him, and had taken his prayers for healing to God. He urged the men to praise and thank God, and to lead righteous lives.

Tobit and Tobias were alarmed to be in the presence of an archangel, and fell to the ground in fear. But Raphael assured them no harm would befall them. "For I did not come as a favor on my part, but by the will of our God," he said. "Therefore praise him forever. All these days I merely appeared to you and did not eat or drink, but you were seeing a vision. And now give thanks to God, for I am ascending to him who sent me. Write in a book everything that has happened." Raphael vanished.

Raphael continues to minister to healing needs, taking the earnest prayers of humans to God, and responding when assigned. Perhaps he is assisted by a host of other healing angels as well, for those who work as healers attest to a variety of helping angelic beings. Are they other angels, working under Raphael's supervision? Or are they Raphael himself, manifesting in whatever guises are required? Perhaps the answer is both.

### Rosemary's angels

Around the same time that I met Eddie, I was introduced to another English medium, Rosemary Gardner, who told me about her experiences with angels in her healing work. I had some remarkable experiences with her, too.

We were introduced by a mutual friend, Graham Wyley, one of England's leading ghost investigators. I don't believe in coincidences, so I can say that surely the angels orchestrated the event.

I'd taken the train from London down to Exeter, in Devon, to appear on BBC Radio Devon with Graham. My itinerary called for heading further south to Torquay, where I'd made arrangements to interview a family about a haunting experience. At the BBC station, I learned that the family had to cancel, and so I was left with a free day and evening, before having to return to London. After the radio show, I talked with Graham about my angel research.

"I know just the person you need to see," he said, explaining to me Rosemary's talents. "But she's very busy, and I don't know if I can get you an appointment tonight." He called Rosemary and learned that a client had cancelled an appointment that evening. I was booked.

Rosemary lived in the little fishing village of Brixham, tucked onto a cliff on one side of Torbay Bay, looking out to palmy Torquay—the "English Riviera"—on the other side. Graham and his wife, Thelma, also lived in Brixham.

Later that evening, Graham and Thelma dropped me off at Rosemary's home, Lobster Pot Cottage. I was greeted by a tall woman with a serene and beatific presence, and a soft, angelic voice. I relaxed and knew that I was in good hands.

Rosemary escorted me into her cottage. It was warm and inviting. Built in 1640, it featured three small rooms downstairs: a sitting room with fireplace, a dining room and a kitchen. The low ceilings had exposed beams. There was an atmosphere of peace and tranquility, which seemed to be the product of Rosemary herself.

Rosemary fixed me a cup of tea, and we sat down at a little wooden table in the dining room. I handed her my watch, from which she received psychic impressions, and she proceeded to give me a reading.

Over the years, I had been to many psychics, mediums and channelers. The reading that Rosemary gave me was remarkable. It was accurate, but accuracy alone only validates the facts. More important, her reading was permeated with a sensitivity that was as though she truly were seeing things from my eyes. It gave me lots of new insights, and I felt much better.

After the reading, Rosemary gave me a healing. She said a silent prayer for guidance, and then placed her hands on me where directed to do so. I felt surrounded by invisible but loving presences, and heat and energy flowed into me, like I was a battery being recharged. Rosemary told me later that during the healing, she had a vision of a meter, like a gas tank gauge, rising from empty to full. I had been feeling exhausted both physically and emotionally, and her analogy certainly expressed my own sense of having been refreshed and restored.

Rosemary and I became good friends, and visited each other on both sides of the Atlantic. On one occasion, I had what I considered an unusual healing of illness from her. It took place in January, when the weather was cold and damp. I arrived in Brixham feeling a severe respiratory infection seizing hold of me. I was badly congested in head and chest, and feared that my entire stay with Rosemary was going to consist of lying in a sickbed.

Rosemary offered to give me a healing. I agreed, though I doubted that anything would help. After making her prayer for divine guidance, Rosemary placed her hands on my head and then at the base of my throat. These positions were held until she received guidance to cease. Then she took me into the sitting room, where a fire crackled in the fireplace, and tucked me onto the sofa with instructions to take a nap. When I woke up two hours later, most of my congestion was gone, and I was well by the next day. I was amazed. It was the first time I'd ever been cured of something by a laying on of hands.

Rosemary aided people with all kinds of health issues, including serious disorders. She did not diagnose or prescribe, but provided a spiritual healing. The people who came to see her were guided by angelic hands, she said, and they sought her kind of healing in addition to other treatments. Perhaps most of all, they sought the angelic comfort that emanated from her.

Rosemary told me she felt the constant presence of angels in her readings and healings, and also the ongoing presence of her own guardian angel. "When I'm doing my healing, I feel angels draw close," Rosemary said. "They help me with my healing. I'm just a channel. They draw close to give people peace. Peace and love come foremost from God, but he sends angels out to gather around people. I handed my life over to God to be help heal people. I think if you hand your life over to be used in that way, he's going to send you help."

Rosemary had her first awareness of angels in early childhood, spent in Suffolk, Essex, and Hampshire. She was born into a family of psychically talented women. Like her mother and grandmother, she saw angels and the dead, and had premonitions and intuitions about things that were going to happen. If she talked about these experiences to others, she got puzzled or negative reactions, indicating that she was somehow different from most other people. Indeed, she felt different, and it isolated her from others.

Her earliest ambitions were to be either a saint—she read voraciously the literature on the lives of the saints—or to be a healer. The two could be considered complementary, for a healer is truly a saint to the healed.

In choosing her calling, Rosemary spent part of her life learning what all true healers must learn: they must heal themselves of their own wounds before they can heal the wounds of others. So, life dealt Rosemary a series of hardships: illness and operations, a near-death experience, two failed marriages, loneliness, financial hardship, loss of friends and family, and her mother's death from cancer.

Rosemary's near-death experience happened when she was in her early twenties. She was married with two small sons, and was working in a children's home. She was stricken with appendicitis and taken to a hospital for surgery.

"The next morning after I'd had the operation, a nurse came in and told me to sit on a chair because she had to make the bed. I wasn't feeling all that well, but I did as I was told. I felt very ill. I decided to go back and lie down on the bed again. I hoped I wouldn't get into trouble from the nurse. I just got back on the bed, and it was just as if I'd passed out. I became aware of myself. I couldn't see anything. I could hear voices around me. It was as if I floated out of my body and could look down at what was going on. There was a bit of a panic, and doctors and nurses were doing something around my bedside. I thought I must be dying.

"Because my sons were very little, and there were these little children at the children's home to look after, I had a horrible thought about leaving them behind. I said prayers: 'Please don't let me die. Not for me, but for them. Just keep me alive long enough so I can bring my children up and look after this and that.

"I floated above the bed. Then I felt as though I was being drawn up a tunnel. It was the most beautiful experience. You couldn't experience anything like it on this earth. At the end of the tunnel was beauty, light, a beautiful white light, and this terrific feeling of love and paradise— something that we just don't experience here on earth. As I started to go up this tunnel, I knew I was leaving my life, and suddenly it didn't worry me. I didn't think I had to go back.

"About halfway up the tunnel, a voice said to me, 'You've got to go back now. You're not meant to come, you've got to go back.' It seemed like it was my guardian angel. I said, 'But I don't want to go back!' I felt this terrific desire to go up to paradise. But the angel said, 'No, you've got to come back, now.'

"Suddenly I was back. I woke up in the bed. I could hear the nurses talking and saying my name, but I couldn't open my eyes. And they said, 'Don't say anything about it, because ignorance is bliss.' When I came out of it, I knew something happened, but they didn't want to talk about it. The doctors and nurses kept coming up and checking me. I thought I must have stopped breathing and they resuscitated me. But it was sort of hushed up.

Rosemary said that as a result of her near-death experience, she would never be frightened of dying. "Death was an unknown before that. But now I would say to anyone, never be afraid of dying, because it is the most beautiful experience. Life is the endurance test, and when we cross over, that's when we go to heaven, and it is a very beautiful place."

One odd circumstance about Rosemary's NDE is that since childhood, she'd had a premonition that she would die young. Sometime after her brush with death, she visited a clairvoyant who looked at her palm.

"This is very strange!" the woman said. "Your hand says you should have died by now. But you're still here!"

Rosemary confirmed her childhood premonition, and her NDE. Her only conclusion was that she had a purpose yet to fulfill—perhaps a purpose that changed her original destiny.

Prior to engaging in her work as a clairvoyant, medium and healer, Rosemary worked in hospitals as an aide. She often was aware of the presence of angels attending to the sick and dying.

On one occasion, while working at a hospital in Hawkhurst, she escorted a group of patients on an outing to the theater. During the performance, an elderly man collapsed of a heart attack. Rosemary helped him into a wheelchair and called for an ambulance. His condition deteriorated so rapidly that she had to get him out of the chair and onto the ground so that she could do mouth-to-mouth resuscitation. When the ambulance arrived, Rosemary sat in the back with him and held his hand. He was unconscious, but she had a sense that being with him and holding his hand provided him reassurance. She was also aware of angelic presences accompanying them on the trip. They were very close, and closing in tighter as the ambulance traveled. She closed her eyes and concentrated on providing comfort.

The man died before the ambulance could reach the hospital. Rosemary was still clasping his hand when one of the attendants opened the ambulance door and gently took her hand away. "He's passed over now," the attendant said.

Three nights later, a presence beside Rosemary's bed awoke her from sleep. It was the elderly gentleman. Rosemary could see him plainly, as though he were still alive. He was radiating warmth and love. He had come to give her a message, which she received as a thought impression.

"Thank you," he said.

Rosemary was well into adulthood before she was ready to work with others to give spiritual healing. In hindsight, she realized that she had to undergo trials and traumas so that she would understand the problems of others, and be able to help them.

"When I've gone through difficult times, I've asked God, why has this happened to me," she said. "The answer comes back that one is never left alone, but you're not protected from all bad things. I've been pushed to the limits of my endurance, to the point where I didn't think I could stand much more. I was told I had to undergo these experiences so I would learn, in order to be able to help others. I had to learn the lesson of forgiveness, that no matter what people do, you forgive them. And I found that God is always with me.

"I asked him, what is the work I have to do? The answer came back that I had to lead people to God. That was the work. I then began to see the reasons for my experiences, that through them I had gotten to a new level of awareness that was enabling me to grow in a spiritual way. As my awareness grew, I could see people around me being presented with lessons, and I could see whether they rejected the lessons or accepted them. And I could see how I was being used in different circumstances to help others.

"God sends suffering so that we can progress and grow spiritually. If we have a life that is easy and comfortable, at the end of it we haven't learned anything. If we have a life that has difficulties in it, then we have the chance to learn from them on the positive side.

"I've found that when people come to see me for help, almost everything they've been through, I've been through. I can immediately identify with them and say yes, I know what it's like. I've been there. That produces compassion. Whereas before, I would have been sympathetic, but I wouldn't have fully understood their problems. The only way to fully understand is to actually be there yourself."

Rosemary continued, "The more difficulties you have, the more you test your faith. The more it's tested, the stronger it gets. When I look at my life, there's a loneliness. There has always been an aloneness from childhood. But the more alone you are, the more you have to turn to God for your needs. When everything is taken away, and you are in very bad difficulties, the only person you can turn to is God, and you find him within."

To develop her psychic and healing abilities, she studied with a Spiritualist medium until he told her he could do no more for her, and she then ventured out on her own. At first, clients were a trickle of friends, and then word of mouth gained her more attention. There were articles in the press, and people from all over England began seeking her out. She then began traveling to America, where she enjoyed immediate success.

Spirit presences manifested when she did a reading or a healing. Some were souls of the dead, such as family members of the client. Some were guardian angels attached to the client, and some were angels who had come to assist with the healing.

The angels were accompanied by a pure, beautiful aura of silver-white light. It was a healing light, and it manifested as Rosemary placed her hands on the client, and flowed through her hands into the person. Usually Rosemary would become aware of an angel—or angels—standing beside her and the client. The awareness was through her inner eye, for Rosemary worked with her eyes shut.

"I do see them," Rosemary told me. "They appear not as a man or a lady, but in a sort of long white robe with fair hair. They have a white aura all around them. I find that if I tell the person that they're not alone, but that angels are always with them, it helps them a lot. Angels are something that they can identify with. Most people want very much to feel that there is a spiritual presence close to them."

Once a woman came to see Rosemary fraught with anxieties over situations in her life. Rosemary gave her a reading and healing, and felt the strong silvery-white light flow through her. The woman, who was sitting with her eyes closed, said, "It's strange, but I can feel an overwhelming sense of peace."

"There's an angel right by you, that's why," responded Rosemary.

"An angel?"

"Your guardian angel," Rosemary said. Then she opened her eyes and looked at the woman. To her surprise, the woman's face was illuminated and transformed. When she had arrived for her appointment, her features had been pinched and drawn with anxiety. Now they were full and serene, and a beautiful, angelic expression graced them.

After that, Rosemary often saw facial transfigurations during healings. "The whole basis of healing is to touch the soul," she said. "We're brought into this life, basically, to find God and to find ourselves in a spiritual life. When one gives healing, it's a direct link with God and angels—who are superior beings—to touch the soul of the person so that they start to grow in a spiritual way. If a person lives a materialistic life, at the end of the day, their soul passes on and they can't take their material things with them. So, if they don't develop in a spiritual way, it's a wasted life. Then they have to come back again to another life.

"If I can give a person an inner peace, and also show them that they're not alone, that's one of the greatest gifts I can give. I give healing with that intent first and foremost. Then I'm helping to heal the mind, and sometimes the physical heals from that. Our Lord Jesus is the finest example of a healer. He healed spiritually, healed minds, and healed bodies, as well."

I asked Rosemary to describe some of her healings with others.

"A lady came to see me who suffered from a loss of balance, and congestion down one side of her head," she said. "I gave her healing, and she became very peaceful and serene and said she felt a lot better. Two days later she rang me up and said, 'You know, I'm feeling so much better, you put everything right.' Then her husband came to see me, and they both came back to see me. He said he was very pleased what had been done for his wife. I thought it was the lovely angelic presence that achieved that, not me.

"Another lady had a lack of mobility in her hands, and lumps on her knuckles. She was going to have an operation in hospital. I said a little prayer to help her, and gave her some healing. I was guided to work from the elbows to the wrists to the hands. Her hands were red. Afterwards there were little dents on one hand where the lumps had gone down, and both hands were a nice pale color, instead of being red. The mobility came back, so that she could use the fingers."

Rosemary went on, "Another lady came to me for a reading. She said, 'I feel I am at a turning point in my life, meeting you. It has made me look at everything in a completely different way.' Readings really help someone find their pathway. People often get to a stage in life and think that there's got to be more to life than this, or which way do they turn— they're searching. The reading helped this lady onto the right pathway. I also gave her some healing for back problems she'd had for years. Later she rang me up and said that two days after having the healing, her back problems were gone, like a miracle.

"Another lady came in a state of depression and anxiety, really awful turmoil. After healing, she said she had a feeling of peace. Although we couldn't change the circumstances of the difficult marriage that she was in, the healing did help her cope. She came back to see me two weeks later and told me she felt as if I'd been with her the whole two weeks. 'You didn't just pick me up and put me back on the pathway, you walked around by the side of me and held my hands,' she said. She explained that she went home from the healing, and because she felt so different, she was different with her husband, and in turn, he responded to her, and in turn, their daughter was happier. So the whole family unit became happy.

"I think everyone has a little candle inside of them," Rosemary said. "I helped to light one in her, and then she went home and lit another one in somebody else, and it spreads. It doesn't just stop at the individual healing. That person will be different, and it will either spread through their family or through their friends.

"You know, it's nice to physically heal. So you make somebody's arm better. Perhaps it just stops there. But people can cope with their physical ailments. For spiritual benefit, they must understand the reasons why they've got them, and the lessons they've got to learn as a result. Then they can basically go on and spiritually help other people. I've had a lot of people come to me who have had healing gifts handed to them, and I've been able to help them, send them out to do more good works. From one little candle, you can light a lot of lights."

Rosemary said healing can be accomplished in many different ways, and that everyone has at least some ability for healing others. "You can heal people by talking to them, even on the phone. Sometimes by just being with them. You can write them a letter. You don't always have to lay hands on somebody.

"People who have come to see me, and are facing difficulties in life, have often said to me they could hear me talking to them in times of need, as though I were actually there with them. The angels take the healing to the people, wherever they are, as it's needed, even in the night while they sleep. It's one of their many missions."

# 9

# Ken Cohen and Spirit Powers of the Native American Way

Kenneth S. Cohen, also known as Ken Bearhawk, is a renowned healer who lives in a log cabin in Nederland, in the mountains of Colorado. Ken is trained in several healing modalities, among them Native American and African healing, and Qigong; he is a Qigong Grandmaster. He has won many awards for his outstanding work in healing and energy medicine.

In his work with Native American healing methods, Ken is aided by animal totems, which are spirit guides or helpers. Totems are similar to angels. Their purpose is to help the spiritual development of a person, and to provide sources of spiritual and psychic power. They dwell within the body rather than externally. Unlike the guardian angel, who comes in at birth and stays until death, totems change during the course of a person's life, depending on spiritual development and needs.

In the Native American tradition, there are various ways that a person can find his or her path of power. The primary one is hereditary. Another is through transference of power by an elder or medicine person. Another is through training. Ken is not Native American by birth, though he feels a profound connection to the Native American path. He has developed his healing power for more than twenty years by training and transference.

He was apprenticed to the Cherokee spiritual teacher, Keetoowah Kristy, the great-grandson of Ned Kristy, a Cherokee hero. Keetoowah Kristy transferred power into Ken's body by using a quartz crystal, which became part of his blood and his being. The use of crystal to transfer medicine power is common in shamanic cultures. Crystal is light made visible, and represents the balance point between two worlds, the seen and the unseen, the material and the spiritual.

Ken also has been initiated into the Seneca's Wolf Clan Teaching Lodge by Grandmother Twyla Nitch (whose name means "She Whose Voice Rides On The Wind), and into the Eagle Tribe and Medicine Society by War Eagle, a Cherokee elder. He has close ties to the Cree in Canada.

I asked Ken to describe his healing methods, and to tell me about some of his experiences with totems.

"In healing, the first thing I do is counsel with the person to get a sense of their situation. That way I can determine whether I have an ability to help them. A good healer knows his strengths and limitations. There are people who come to me who I cannot help, and I make referrals. If I determine that they have a problem that I can address, especially if it is spiritual in origin, then I wait a couple of days to see if I receive guidance from my spirit helpers. Then I meet with the person again, and start. I consider everything I do as complementary therapy instead of alternative therapy.

"In working with patients, first I purify them by smudging, which is using the smoke from burning sage. Some use sweet grass or cedar. I might see more about their illness through the smoke.

"I use a lot of prayer, opening myself to a transpersonal source of power. I feel that when I do healing, it is not coming from me, but is moving through me. I am able to connect to the Great Mystery, the Creator, who does the healing.

"I do a lot of noncontact healing, in which I visualize, energy passing through my hands to the person. Occasionally, the healing work will take the form of my placing sacred stones on their bodies. The stones have their own healing natures, and are tuned through my prayer.

"There are various spiritual techniques that might be required in particular cases. For instance, I might see that a source of a person's problem is that they are out of touch with their spirit guides, their totems. If I sense that is the case, or the spirit helper has left, or the connection to the person is very tenuous, I perform a healing ceremony to re-establish contact. That can be done through prayer and calling songs that invoke the presence of a particular helper. It can also be done by waving the person's spirit helper back into the body with a feather fan, or using the breath to blow the helper back into the body. Occasionally I've asked a plant, such as tobacco, which is sacred, to help me with this. I take the tobacco smoke in my mouth and blow the spirit helper back to the body with the smoke."

"How do you compare spirit helpers to angels?" I asked.

"I think they are basically the same," Ken answered. "A more interesting question is whether these helpers or angels are the same as the unconscious. I think the boundary between inside and outside is an imaginary one. It's a boundary of concepts, not something we actually experience. When a person is deeply in touch with himself and is practicing what Carl Jung called creative imagination, the guides that come out of the unconscious are the same as the spirit powers. On the other hand, if a person contacts the spirit powers, that is the same as reaching into the unconscious. The unconscious is not within the body—it's the other way around. The body is within the unconscious. Spirit helpers or angels are part of the collective us.

"In Native American culture, there are different ways to conceptualize the helpers, all of whom are messengers for, and aspects of, the Great Mystery. In the Seneca Wolf Clan Teaching Lodge, Grandmother Twyla speaks about four spirit band members, who are guides who tend to appear in human form. My own visions tell me that these four band members represent the four directions, each with its own teaching. A person might not recognize or work with all of them at the same time. You might go through certain experiences in your life that help you to become aware of one particular band member, for example, the east, which is the direction of inspiration and creativity, and having the wide, panoramic vision of the eagle. After some time, you might become aware of the band members in other directions. It could take a year, it could take ten years, it could take twenty years to learn all four—it's an individual process.

"In my work, I've discovered that most people have two totem animals, who are in addition to the human-like four band members. The totems represent the conscious and the unconscious—the obvious aspect and a more hidden aspect of one's self. All—totems and band members—

are sources of knowledge and wisdom. One can learn to dialogue with them, in a way analogous to the process of creative imagination. They are also actual sources of power, because they are intermediaries between the physical world and the Creator, the Great Mystery. They can be sources of power channeling. Perhaps 'funneling' is a better word. They funneling power down to us when it's needed. In shamanic cultures, if you lose touch with your power, whether it be a totem or a band member or some combination of the two, then you are vulnerable to misfortune and disease. A healing is necessary to re-establishing that contact, and restore power and vitality."

"How do we lose touch with our power?" I asked.

"We lose touch with our power through not following our original instructions—our assignment that the Great Mystery has written in our hearts," Ken said. "In other words, we lose touch by not having the courage to be fully ourselves and to follow the promptings that come from inside, and instead we're false to our medicine. For instance, we are not true to our medicine if we live our lives according to other people's expectations, or the conditioning influences of educational and religious institutions. We also can be disrespectful to our medicine. For instance, if someone has a particular gift to be an artist, poet, or singer, and they don't allow themselves to express that gift, they are disrespectful to their medicine, and they become sick.

"A good example is a woman I worked with one time. I felt she had a great deal of sensitivity to people and their feelings, and that this could have been turned into a real advantage in her life. She could have been a wonderful therapist. But she had so little confidence in herself because of an abusive childhood that she never allowed herself to follow what she really felt should have been her authentic lifestyle or career. So she took up a job in business and became a manager. She didn't hate her work, but she always had an unfulfilled need to work with other people. Her sickness was chronic fatigue syndrome, which she has suffered for many years.

"When I looked at her, I saw that she had a deer and an eagle around her. Very clearly. This made sense to her—these were symbols that were relevant to her. I told her the deer was her sensitivity to energy, and the eagle was her penetrating vision or ability to look through the shells, through the masks that people use to project their social roles. She could see through that to what was authentic underneath. She began to work with those totem powers and as a result, the chronic fatigue syndrome lessened its hold on her. So, working with the spirit powers can have a very concrete effect on a person's personality and health."

"Were her totems comparable to guardian angels?" I asked.

"Yes, although totems change in the course of one's life. Sometimes new spirit powers will seek to come in to further growth and development, but a person will not make the life changes necessary to allow them in. The person will sometimes go through illness, which is due to the fact that the old spirit power has left, but the person has not made himself a fit receptacle for the new spirit power that wants to come in.

"I'll give you another example of this kind of shielding. I had a student who was a street person. He panhandled for money, slept in abandoned cars in junkyards in the winter time or slept out on the streets with drug addicts. He used to hang around classes I taught, but he never seemed to be quite 'there.' He looked like a burned out hippie left over from the sixties. One time he came to me and said, 'I know I have problems and I want to change. What can I do?' It was the first time he had ever spoken coherently to me.

"I told him that the first step in any kind of healing is that the person has to ask to be healed. If they don't ask, nothing can be done for them. That is why healers will often ask for some kind of donation or an offering. I personally don't feel that it's right to put a monetary value on healing, but if the person doesn't give anything, then you know that they're not really asking for anything. Maybe they're just looking for a way to feel more comfortable with their problems, or they're curious, or they want entertainment or a new way to get high.

"This man really wanted to change. I asked him what he felt was his problem. He said he had no willpower. He said that whenever anyone offered him drugs or anything he could get high on, he would take them right away. 'Do you really want to stop?' I said. He said, 'Yes.' I said, I'll tell you what you do. You cut off an inch of your hair and you burn it outside. And you say, Creator, I don't have anything. All I have is my own body. I'm offering this to you as a sign, as a release that I want something to change in my life.' I explained to him that this would be enough of an offering for me. I also said to him, 'Find some place where you can take a bath. Go to one of the hot tubs somewhere, and get a new set of clothes. I don't care where you get them, from the Salvation Army or wherever, but put them through the laundry and get them clean as possible. When you've taken a bath and made that offering of your hair and found new clothes, then come up to my cabin and I'll be willing to work with you.'

"He did all that, and four days later he came up to the cabin. I did a ceremony over him, smudging him and then praying over him. When I looked at him spiritually, I saw the most extraordinary thing: an eagle that was above his body. Now normally if someone is in touch with their spirit power, I can see it in their heart, but his spirit power was definitely removed and was outside of his body. On the face of the eagle there was a mask, a human face of evil intent. I used a feather to take the mask off and to discharge it. After I removed the mask, I made a prayer to the Great Mystery. I said, 'You know what is best to do with these things. We don't send them back to the ones who send them. If this mask was put on my brother here intentionally, then you know what is best to do with it.' That's that way I was taught—never send anything bad to somebody else. There are people who think that if someone can put something evil on another person, it should be sent back to them. I was taught to give it to the Creator instead.

"When I took the mask off, I could see the eagle's natural face underneath. I shook that eagle back into my student's heart until it was resting there. When the ceremony was over, my student looked like a different person. His eyes could focus. Before that time, for all the months I had seen him in my class, his eyes could not track—they would wander all over the place. He couldn't speak more than a few words coherently, and after that could only manage broken fragments of a sentence. Now he looked like a normal human being.

"When I spoke to him about the face that I saw on the mask, it turned out that face was the exact description of someone he used to live with, some ten or more years before, in New York City. This person was apparently involved in some sort of satanic cult. My student said that it was after he left that person's home that everything went downhill in his life. He lost his job, his friends, he got divorced, he never saw his children again. He began to live out on the streets. He eventually found his way to Colorado. I felt he was indeed hexed, and it was a combination of his own weakness and that other person's bad intent.

"After he had his spirit power restored, he was a different person. Within two weeks, he had a place to live, and he had gotten a job as an apprentice to a landscape gardener. He stopped taking drugs. He became very stable. In fact, he became my best student.

"To sum it up," said Ken, "The spirit powers are helpers and messengers, and they usually come to us as a grace. Our training can invite their presence, but we can't specifically stalk or track a particular power. We can only make ourselves open to it. What my elders have always told me is that the most important power, the highest power, and the one which people must always keep central in their lives—especially if they're working with the spirit powers—is the Creator, or God."

"How do we open ourselves to the spirit powers?"

"The first thing is to find out what animal you have an affinity with," Ken responded. "Some people just know that. They know that because of their dreams, or because of feelings they have when they see a certain animal—they feel like singing and dancing. If a person does not know intuitively what his totem animals are, it probably means he has not spent enough time in nature. There is no substitute for that. It's not enough to simply do guided imagery work and to imagine a situation where an animal can come to you. I feel a person must physically go out and be in nature. When you live close to nature, then these spirit animal presences, as well as the physical animals, make themselves known.

"I can give you another example of this as well. I had a client who felt victimized at work. Her boss didn't like her, and she felt her boss tried to turn other people against her. She just couldn't stand it, and she wanted to get a transfer to a different office. But that was up to her boss, who hated her anyway, and she just felt trapped. When I asked her what animal she felt closest to, she said cats. As soon as she said it, I saw a mountain lion. I asked her how she felt about mountain lions, and she said she loved them. I knew I was on the mark.

"I said, 'All right, the mountain lion is a hunter—it is not the hunted. The mountain lion can be invisible. When you go to work this week, I want you to imagine that you are a mountain lion and that way you will not be a victim. Your boss will not notice you, or your boss will be so scared of your power that he will not say anything bad against you. Let me know what happens as a result.'

"I saw her again two weeks later. She told me she had been transferred to a different office. During the time that she was doing her visualization as a mountain lion, her boss did not notice her and did not make any rude remarks. She felt a radical difference in her health and her spirit. She was very happy with the new place and new employees she was working with."

Ken continued, "It's not only important to invite the spirit presences in, it's also important to honor them and express gratitude to them. Honoring and gratitude are the reasons for Native American songs and dances. You can go out into nature, some place where you can be alone, and sing a song to your animal, dance it, or move like it. Some people draw a painting as a way of honoring their totems. Find some way to express gratitude, because any power or gift that you are grateful for then becomes stronger in you."

"Is prayer a good way to do that?"

"Prayer is very, very important. In the West, we think of prayer as asking for something. That can be part of prayer, but the most important aspect from the Native perspective is expressing gratitude—for the gift of life, for one's family, for the land, for the air, for the water, the food, for all the things that sustain us. We have to remember that there are also spiritual forces that sustain us—the Great Mystery and the various spirit helpers."

"How have you come into contact with your own spirit helpers?" I wanted to know.

Ken answered, "In 1977, I was passing through Colorado on my way to California, and one day while I was taking a walk in the city there was a tremendous storm. In this area of the country, there are usually afternoon thunderstorms in the summertime, and they clear up after about an hour or two, sometimes with spectacular rainbows. This storm seemed to come from one mountain of clouds that was formed in such a perfect shape it looked like an actual mountain that was generating the lightning and thunder. This experience seemed to be a message or an omen. That night, when I went to sleep, I prayed and asked for the meaning of the vision of the storm clouds. Suddenly I sat up. I was still awake. I looked outside the window of the house to two pine trees. I saw, very clearly, two beings, one seated on each of the pine trees. On the pine tree to the left there was a red shadow. On the pine tree to the right, there was a large black thunderbird. It looked almost like an eagle, but it was about nine feet long. Both of these beings communicated to me mentally. They said they were messengers that had been sent to bring me to that mountain that I saw. The next day, I should buy a pair of deer skin moccasins, take my sacred pipe and travel west. The pipe, by the way, is a medium of prayer used in many of the Native American tribes. Natural tobacco and herbs are smoked and sent up with one's breath to the Great Mystery.

"I did as instructed the next day. I travelled through a small town, where I'm now living, and on to the top of the Continental Divide. When I got up there, at about 11,000 or so feet, I saw the exact, real mountain that I had seen formed by the shape of the clouds the day before. There was an alpine lake. I knew that was the place I was supposed to be in. I prayed in gratitude while I was up there. This has been my special place in the world ever since.

"I went on to live in California for about four years. In 1981, I went through a difficult time emotionally, and was about to start a divorce process. I knew that some physical change was needed as well and I should move, and live away from the city. One evening I was doing inner work, and a woman appeared in my mind. She was a Native American, dressed in white buckskin, and was extraordinarily beautiful. She had energy pouring out of her palms. I saw that she had an amulet that looked like a huge mirror hanging around her neck. I knew I was supposed to look into that mirror. When I looked, I saw again the mountain that I had visited in 1977. I knew that I was supposed to live there, and this was a message for me to move there. Whatever I needed to be brought into my life, or needed to release in terms of the pain and sorrow I was going through in the divorce, somehow all these things would come to me more easily if I was living near that mountain. So I moved within a short period of time.

"In 1984, exactly seven years from the time I had first visited that holy place, I went there on a formal vision quest. I was living in my present home, a log cabin which is about a four-hour hike to the alpine lake. I undertook the vision quest to find new meaning or direction in my life. I had gone through the divorce, I felt I was at a turning point spiritually, and the Native American spirituality was becoming much more central in the way I was living.

"As I was hiking up to the lake, something very strange happened. I experienced extreme, excruciating pain in my hip, such that I could hardly walk. I could hardly move. By the time I got to the lake, I was just dragging myself along. Storm clouds had been gathering, and once I got myself up there, thunder began to rumble. I put up my tent. The moment it was up, a terrific hail storm started. The hailstones looked like golf balls.

I was worried they were going to rip the tent apart. I was quite frightened. But I had so much pain in my body that I felt that I could not hike down from that place. Now, it was late May, very early in the season to be in such high country, and there were no other hikers or people around. I decided to take out my pipe and to ask for the meaning of this experience. And the moment I put the bowl and the stem together, the storm stopped, and a ray of light shone down on my tent. I stepped outside and there was a small eagle seated on a branch of a tree about fifteen feet away from me. The eagle took off flying to the east. I heard a voice in my mind that said, 'Now you are like the small eagle flying to the east, but soon you will be like us. Look up.' I looked up and there were two eagles circling overhead. Again I heard in my mind a voice that said, 'Always remember, there is no virtue in suffering. Only follow the way of the pipe.' It repeated itself. 'Always remember there is no virtue in suffering. Always follow the way of the pipe.' That message has stayed with me. For me, following the way of the pipe is finding a way to live that makes me as much like the pipe as possible and much like a clear channel, dedicated to the Great Mystery so the breath of the Great Mystery can move through me. It is part of my life, part of my every action. That's my dedication. My commitment.

"Seven years later, in 1991, I visited the lake again. There were no visits in between. This is a sacred place for me and out of respect for that place, I only go when the need is there. Interestingly, this has been every seven years. In 1991, an inner voice told me I must go back to that mountain just to express gratitude that over the past seven years, I had been blessed with wonderful teachers and had been able to follow more closely my commitment.

"When I went back to the mountain, I had a feeling of total clarity up there. The first two times I had been there, in 1977 and 1984, the sky was dark and stormy. In 1991, I was going there to express gratitude for the clarity that I had felt in my life for seven years, and for the teachers and the wonderful elders that I've been blessed to work with. The sky was totally clear, and the lake water was sparkling in the most unusual way, like glittering diamonds.

"I offered my pipe to send the smoke out to the directions. Right after I finished blowing the smoke, the eagle called two times. I don't know if it was the same eagle calling twice or two eagles calling one after the other. But I knew this was an affirmation from that same power I had seen seven years earlier in my vision quest, when the two eagles had flown overhead and they had told me that I would soon be like them, just follow the way of the pipe. These eagles had stayed with me. They have given me other affirmations as well.

"Recently I went to Nevada to visit one of my dear elders and friends, Rolling Thunder, and to live in his camp. While I was there, I was going to offer a pipe ceremony in his honor. Just before the ceremony, a triple rainbow appeared, extending out over the desert. Beautiful! A golden eagle flew right under the arch of the rainbow. Then, a few days ago, I was up at the top of Mt. Evans here in Colorado, and got about five feet away from a mountain goat. I sat watching this mountain goat feeding for a long time, and had a wonderful feeling of communion with it. I offered the goat a little bit of tobacco in gratitude. Just as I did so, I felt something over my head, and sure enough there was an eagle circling way up overhead. So, these experiences with the eagles have been repeating themselves. You know, the elders teach us that we are not supposed to try to get the medicine. There's too much greed in the world already. In spiritual matters, we have to have the dedication, and instead of us choosing the medicine, the medicine will choose us."

"Are you aware of the eagles when you perform a healing?" I asked.

"Sometimes, yes," Ken said. The eagle will help. Sometimes I might visualize an eagle over a person's body, fanning them. Healing depends on what kind of power is compatible with a person. I don't use a power that is incompatible with their own spirit power. I first listen to what the person has to say about their situations, and try to ascertain what kind of spirit power they are working with."

Ken said that his guide told him he would visit his holy mountain four times. "In the Native American traditions, things happen in multiples of four or seven. Four is a number of hope—it's a quaternity, completeness in four directions. Seven is also a number of wholeness. It can imply the four directions and the three periods of time: past, present and future, and so it embraces space and time all together. Seven is a medicine number that is revered by most Native American tribes. In fact, the number seven is so important that in some of the Cherokee ways of working with medicine, the number is said at the end of an invocation."

I asked Ken if the woman in white buckskin had appeared to him again.

"She has appeared a couple of times, but never with the same impact as that first time. I think there has not been the need on my part. I feel that the more you make your mind one with the Great Mystery and the spirits, the more you open yourself to them, and the helpers become part your life. You don't have to use specific means to retrieve information."

Ken told me about another of his experiences involving an owl as a spirit helper. "The owl is a spirit that many Native people have a somewhat ambivalent relationship with," he said. "For instance, certain tribes will not work with the owl at all because they consider it a bringer of misfortune. Other tribes definitely feel that the owl is a helper. The owl is nocturnal. For me this association with the night gives the owl the significance of death and rebirth. I don't necessarily mean physical death and rebirth—it can be spiritual death and rebirth. In other words, dying to something that you don't need in your life anymore, making room for something that is new, that you do need.

"I had an experience with the owl when I went through a healing crisis a number of years back. I had an infection in one of my heart valves. One of my students, not knowing that I was ill, called me and asked me if I was all right. She said she'd had a frightening dream about me, in which an owl came and took my heart out of my chest, held it in his talons and took two bites out of it and started flying to the north.

"I immediately knew that I had only four days left to live, I don't know how I knew it was four days, but somehow I just knew. My symptoms had been worsening. I had extreme pressure in the center of my chest. I couldn't walk more than a block without getting out of breath. I had pain. I was waking up in the middle of the night with severe pains in the chest. I had a generally ominous feeling about my health.

"We immediately had a ceremony in which the dreamer, the woman who called me, led it, following instructions I gave her, because she was not a Native shaman herself. She was supported by other friends, both Native and non-Native. The object of the ceremony was to invite this owl to come back from the north. Otherwise, I knew that if he got to the extreme north, I would be gone. I would cross over.

"The ceremony was successful. We asked the owl to return to spit out the pieces it had swallowed, to mend the heart and to put it back in my chest. The owl did this. Immediately after the ceremony—and I mean immediately—all my symptoms were gone. My blood pressure, which had been way up, was down to normal, the pressure in my chest was gone. My vitality was back to normal. I was feeling fine. Earlier, an echocardiogram done at the hospital had shown I had an extreme collapse of the mitral valve with some regurgitation of blood back into the atrium. The morning after the ceremony, I felt there was a structural change in my heart. I haven't had another echocardiogram done, but I have had a physician listen to my heart. There is no telltale clicking sound, unless I'm under stress."

"How did this experience influence your view of the owl?"

"I would say that the owl is a messenger of the night-time, and a messenger of transition. Something that helps one go through the dark night of the soul. The owl also can be a guide into the afterlife. It can be a symbol of death. For me, it was a potential symbol of death, but became a symbol of transition."

I thanked Ken for sharing his experiences. I saw many parallels in the ways that angels work and the ways that spirit helpers work. They all come from the same source, God, or the Great Mystery.

"Working with angels or spirit powers should not be the object of one's spirituality," Ken cautioned. "These are merely helpers, and one's devotion has to be fixed on the Great Mystery, the Creator. If I meet someone who speaks too much about powers or presences, I feel they've been sidetracked, or perhaps their motivation is not right. Perhaps they're more interested in power or in the emotional thrill they get out of working with these different helpers. One's dedication really has to be centered all the time on the Great Mystery."

Ken continues his shamanic and healing work from his base in Nederland, Colorado.

# 10

## Working with the Rainbow Bridge
## to Higher Consciousness

Thus far we've seen the many ways that angels manifest to people. They respond to request, prayer, and need, and they act as an interface with the Godhead. Those who experience angels, especially in a dramatic way, feel transformed and changed, especially in their spiritual outlook.

Angels are far more complex than meeting urgent needs, however, and serve as a guide and a bridge to the development of spiritual consciousness. They can be accessed on a daily basis, a contact which stimulates an ongoing process of change and transformation for the individual. How can we work with angels in this way?

### Meditation and prayer

Meditation and prayer are two of the most effective ways to communicate with and comprehend angels. You don't need to have a dire problem. A daily meditation habit is desirable for any spiritual pursuit, even involvement in paranormal investigations and activities, as I often counsel people in those fields. Spending just a few minutes a day centering and attuning to the spiritual planes has a powerful cumulative effect. It refines consciousness and thought, where manifestation in physical reality begin. As you think, so you are, and so you live.

There are many ways to meditate. Years ago, I was a member of a zendo and learned Zen meditation, which I still practice in an adapted form today. However, you need not adhere to a formal training system—you can meditate in simple ways, anywhere, anytime. At home, sit quietly and relax the body, and practice letting go of distracting thoughts. It is impossible to stop thinking altogether, but it is possible to minimize the busy mind. Let distracting thoughts go like water through a sieve, or let them float away like balloons.

When you feel very still and relaxed, make a mental connection to the Godhead, however you perceive it, and then ask for the angels who are close to you, including your guardians, to be present and make themselves known to you.

You may feel a distinct shift in the environment around you, including a sense of presences. You may feel a mental connection and "hear" words in your mind. Angels make themselves known in the ways that are best for each individual.

As noted earlier, names are calling cards in the spiritual planes, and so allowing names to come through is important. Angel names can be simple or exotic. Not every angel has to have a Biblical-sounding name. Remember LNO and Silver Lady?

In meditation, you can also ask angels questions for guidance, or you can simply sit in the angelic presence, absorbing the energy on an intuitive level.

Over time, you will notice changes, some subtle and some dramatic. Angelic guidance and presence will be presented to you in many ways, including synchronicity, intuition, dreams, signs in the environment, words and actions from other people, and an inner "knowing." If you look at yourself from the perspective of an instrument, you will become more finely tuned to the "music of the spheres," the subtle vibrations that flow all the time through all things in creation.

You will find yourself thinking and living differently than you did in the past. You will find yourself having more energy, thinking more clearly, and possessing a greater ability to stay focused. Meditation also benefits the body and overall health.

I recommend starting the day with meditation, and it is also a good way to end the day. There is no excuse for not having enough time before rushing out to work. Set the alarm a little earlier. If something is important enough, you make the time for it, don't you?

In addition, you can do mini-meditations anywhere: taking a break at work, sitting on a plane, train, or bus, or standing in line. You should not attempt to meditate, of course, while driving.

Angels have key attributes that provide different perspectives for meditation and contemplation. By focusing on them individually, it is possible to tap deeper into the mystery of angels and their power.

## The rainbow bridge

As intercessors between humanity and the Godhead, angels literally are a bridge to the heavens and a symbol of higher consciousness. They form a rainbow bridge, one of the most powerful symbols of all in terms of a connection to the Divine.

The popular image of the angel is as a being of dazzling white light, based on many accounts through the ages of encounters with beings bathed in white light, or appearing as balls and pillars of white light.

The true nature of an angel is one of brilliant color. Renaissance artists understood this secret, and painted angels full of color. Their flowing clothing is resplendent in shimmering colors. What's more, the wings of angels are often painted as rainbows. The wings do not necessarily have all the colors of the rainbow, but they are layered and many-hued, with greens, blues, reds, purples, golds, and yellows.

Why is color, and especially a band of colors, significant? In mythologies around the world, the rainbow is a universal symbol of the bridge to the realm of the gods. The rainbow is the path along which walk the souls of the dead as they cross over into the afterlife; it is the road walked by deities and the enlightened to the higher planes of consciousness.

The rainbow is a symbol of God's covenant with people. In Genesis 9:11-17, God sets a rainbow in the heavens after the Flood has receded, as a sign to Noah that God shall never again destroy life on Earth. Whenever a rainbow appears in the sky, it is a reminder of that promise.

Rainbows appear in the literature of angels as well. In 3 Enoch, rainbow arches rest upon the seventh heaven and encircle the Throne of Glory. The throne angels, who bear the seat of God, rest upon the arches.

How appropriate that angels—who are the bridge between heaven and earth, and the means by which we can access the kingdom of God—have rainbow wings.

Even if wings are portrayed as white in art, the garb of angels includes many colors. Images of angels that are full of colors, whether the colors are on the wings, the clothing, or in background detail, signify that the gates to the higher planes of consciousness are open.

## Wings

The wing itself also is a symbol of the bridge to the Godhead. Wings represent spirituality, divine purpose, speed, and the ability to mediate between physical and nonphysical realms. The endowment of wings on spiritual beings is an ancient idea, but one that developed in the West more so than in the East. It is interesting that Eastern deities, saints, and spiritual beings move about through space without the benefit of wings, which technically are not necessary. In art, Eastern deities are shown descending from the sky or hovering in the air, held up by the weightlessness of their own divinity. Western art, on the other hand, has depicted certain gods and semi-divine beings as having wings to denote their special multi-dimensional powers and abilities—wings enable them to reach the heavens.

Earlier, we touched on the development of wings in descriptions of the appearance of angels. The winged angel did not appear significantly in art until about the fourth century AD. Artists then drew on earlier models, such as from Assyria. As early as the ninth century BC, Assyrians began placing wings on the shoulders of their protective entities such as the *kari-bu*, a half-human, half-animal figure that guarded buildings. The ancient Egyptians also used wings, such as on the human-headed bird that represents the *ba*, the eternal part of the soul.

The greatest influences on the winged angel came out of Greek and Roman mythology, specifically the figure of Nike, the winged goddess of victory (called Victoria or Victory by the Romans). To the Romans, Nike/Victory symbolized the invincibility of the Roman Empire, a trait borrowed by the Christians and converted to represent the invincibility of Christ. In art, winged Victory was customarily shown with one breast exposed, and was sometimes depicted naked with a mantle or drapery flowing around her. Her image was adopted into sacred art in Egypt and Syria.

If not for such precedents as these, the early Christian artists would not have had much in the way of models for depicting angels.

The Christian angel was inherited from the Hebrews, who prohibited images of their religious concepts. Thus, the Old Testament gives scant information on the appearance of angels. Seraphim and cherubim are sometimes described as having wings, but otherwise angels "came," "stood" or "went" without details as to how they moved about. Angels appeared as lightning and flame and as human-like beings that passed for mortals. Even the angels of the New Testament are not described as winged. Gabriel, in announcing the birth of Jesus to Mary, merely "comes in" and "departs." The angels who announced the birth of Jesus to the shepherds just appeared "suddenly" and "came upon them" in the night. We are not told if they flew in or walked in.

Early angel artists, limited by scant descriptive information, portrayed angels as ennobled, ethereal male-like humans without wings. Though angels played an important role in Christian piety from a very early stage, it was not until 325 that the Council of Nicea made belief in angels a part of dogma. This stimulated theological discussions and writings on angels, including the matter of angels' flight.

The winged, hovering angel evolved dramatically during the fourth century, creating a formula that dominated art through the sixth century. By the end of the fourth century, Christian artists had turned to pagan gods for inspiration. They borrowed heavily from the Greek idea that divinity has shape and it is human-like, and from the Roman image of Victory. However, they refrained from frank nakedness and sexuality. Their angels were adult males but without pronounced sexual characteristics— almost androgynous in appearance—and were fully clothed with a tunic and mantle. Their wings often were not pronounced in size or detail. By the end of the fifth century, the winged, hovering angel had become common in art.

This formula angel was often shown in pairs, holding a wreath with the medallion of Christ, or wreaths with the cross of Christ, or other ceremonial symbols. Angels were reserved for depiction of the central themes in Christianity and not the daily affairs of humans. These themes underscored the role of angels as divine messengers of God who had several main responsibilities: to execute the will of God; to serve as guardians of, and attendants to, Christ; to be guides of the soul after death to the afterlife; to be important participants in ceremonies; and to be heralds of the Last Judgment.

Over time, angels became more beautiful and endowed with larger and more glorious wings in art. In part, this reflected a decline in theological interest in the angel. Artists thus were freer to be more creative. They began portraying angels as male youths and women. They used birds such as the eagle and swan for models of great wings.

The Renaissance images, so breath-taking and glorious, set the standard for what we today believe angels look like. The wings, symbols of access to higher realms, are large, elegant, and graceful. When we see the wings of angels, we are reminded of our own ability to rise to the higher realms and be closer to God. As we ascend, we are like the Renaissance angel, full of grace and beauty.

## Halos

In art, angels are often depicted with halos. These crowns of light denote divinity or high spiritual consciousness. They represent the crown chakra, which becomes prominent when consciousness is raised to a significant level. Ancient Egyptians, Greeks, Indians, and Romans used the halo in art to depict supernatural force, mystical states, and superior intellect. In ancient Egypt and Greece, the halo was associated with the sun and resurrection. In the Greek Eleusinian Mysteries, a halo was bestowed upon the sacrificed and reborn grain god, usually Dionysus. In Christian art, the halo graces saints, Christ, the Blessed Virgin Mary, and other holy persons, as well as angels. Eastern deities usually are depicted with crowns or headdresses rather than halos, which symbolize the same thing.

Thus we see that the halo has a universal meaning of spiritual enlightenment and resurrection of the spirit to the Light, or Godhead. The halo of the angel tells us that the power to achieve this is within us.

Meditation enhances the flow of the universal life force throughout the body and the aura, including the chakras. Meditation combined with a spiritual path raises more energy into the crown chakra—our own halo. When you meditate on angels, envision absorbing and embodying their spiritual energy.

## Beauty

The angel is a being of great beauty, so grand that to look upon an angel overwhelms us with awe and humility.

There are two key meanings to this ethereal beauty. In art, beauty symbolizes Truth. Truth, with a capital T, is absolute. Understanding Truth is beyond the expression of words. The angel represents the Absolute Truth of God. To comprehend this is a more a mystical experience than one that can be explained by left-brain thinking. Through the angel, we attain knowledge of the cosmos and the unity of all things. We experience unconditional love as the force that creates and binds everything together.

The second key meaning of the angel's beauty is a mirror. Angels, whom we perceive as idealized forms of us, reflect back to us the beauty of our own souls. To gaze upon an angel is to see the reflection of our true essence.

## The angel as mandala

All of these facets of the angel comprise a whole that is like a mandala, which is another way to contemplate angels. The term "mandala" means "circle" in Sanskrit. The mandala is a circular design that expresses ultimate wholeness and makes order out of chaos. The mandala represents the point where macrocosm of the heavens and the microcosm of Earth meet. It symbolizes the journey of life to the Center of All Things—the Great Mystery. The mandala communicates with the ineffable, a consciousness deeper than conceptual thought.

In Eastern mysticism, mandalas can be elaborate geometrical designs that are instruments of contemplation for advancing consciousness (yantras). Everything in them are precise symbols. Deities reside within these forms. These deities are related to the forces existing throughout the mentally created universe.

Mandalas have three basic properties. The first is a center, which signifies the Godhead, the Beginning and the Eternal Now. The second is symmetry, a design that is an arrangement of balanced proportions. The third is an orientation to four cardinal points.

Anything round or with symmetry can be a mandala: the sun, the moon, the earth, a clock, an equilateral cross, the Zodiac, a wheel, a rotunda, a halo, a flower, a maze, a labyrinth, a rose window of a cathedral. Octagons, squares, and triangles suggest mandalas, since circles may be drawn within them or around them.

Mandalas are most strongly associated with Eastern mysticism, but they also appear in Christianity, Gnosticism, other religions, mythology, alchemy, healing practices, art, and architecture. Carl G. Jung observed mandalas in the works of alchemy and in medieval Christian art. He was particularly drawn to depictions of Christ (the Center) surrounded by his four evangelists at the cardinal points. Jung found that the integrative properties of the mandala had benefits in psychotherapy. By drawing mandalas, patients could begin to make order out of their inner chaos.

Mandalas are comparable to archetypes in Western thought. Archetypes express and hold the essence of something, in all its meanings. Archetypes are realized through experience.

Angels are representations of archetypes. They represent the ability of the human soul to ascend to heaven and descend to the underworld. They also represent the immortality and inherent divine nature of the soul. As mandalas, angels help us make order out of our inner chaos.

How exactly can angels be mandalas? Angels do appear as round forms of light, but they are most like a mandala in artistic depictions of them in their winged, human-like form, which has elegant symmetry and cardinal point orientation.

As mentioned above, mandalas all have a center, symmetry, and cardinal points. The angel itself is a center, a representative of the Godhead. The artistic form of the angel, like the body of a human, has symmetry that can be oriented to four cardinal points: the limbs outstretched reach in four directions, and a circle or square can be drawn around such a figure. Think of the famous "Vitruvian Man" drawn by Leonardo da Vinci around 1490. The male figure is shown with limbs outstretched, oriented to the cardinal points of a square and within a circle. Da Vinci based his drawing on the geometry of the Roman architect Vitruvius, who saw the human body as a main source of proportion in architecture. Put wings on the figure and you have the angel, a source of the proportions of cosmic architecture.

Another cardinal orientation of the mandala angel comes from the angel's association with the Four Principles of Love, Truth, Justice, and Immortality. Angels represent the unconditional love of God. They stand for truth and justice in the fight between the forces of light and darkness. And, they symbolize the resurrection of the victorious soul to eternal life.

Like Eastern mandalas, in which small details have specific meanings, the components of the angel also have certain meanings, such as their colors, wings, and halos. In your meditation, you may discover other meaningful details as well. Once you realize how the angel is a mandala of the cosmos, the image of an angel—even the thought of an angel—will automatically trigger a response in your consciousness that aligns you to that spiritual vibration. The angel becomes a charged image that automatically activates information and awareness. You will not have to stop and acknowledge every component, for you will comprehend it in totality and intuitively, understanding at once all the meanings of the individual aspects of the angel and the synergy of the whole.

This approach to working with angels is never static and never reaches an end. It continuously unfolds new and deeper insights. Start now, and discover where the path of angels will take you.

# Epilogue:
# A Path of Light

In the opening chapters of this book, I stated some reasons why we are experiencing a surge in interest in angels, and why we are having more encounters with them. One reason is that whenever we are plunged into turmoil, we turn to spiritual help. Another reason is the existence of a collective spiritual emptiness that cries out for more personal spiritual relationships than those offered by conventional religious channels. Yet another reason is a growing interest in otherworldly experiences of all kinds.

Angels are part of our mythology, and we are attempting to reclaim the riches of our mythological tradition, which have been buried by science and technology. We are in need of great help because we have great problems, on both individual and global scales.

We are multidimensional beings. Throughout history, we have developed worldviews—and the scientific paradigm—that have trapped us into a three-dimensional reality. Our consciousness, however, is not limited to physical reality. Angels dwell in a nonordinary reality, as do other beings from our mythologies. These nonordinary realities have fantastical or dream-like qualities to them, but they that are just as real as the physical world we inhabit. We are able to experience these other realities when openings occur, such as in shifts of consciousness and dreaming, and sometimes being in the right place, such as a sacred site or enchanted land.

Breakthroughs to other realities are on the increase. Media exposure has made public discussion of extraordinary experiences not only acceptable, but desirable. A little more than a century ago, only 10 percent of adults acknowledged having an apparition experience, according to a census published in 1889 by the Society for Psychical Research in London. Today, approximately half the adult population in the United States alone reports some type of apparitional experience, such as ghosts, otherworldly beings, visions of spiritual figures, near-death experiences, out-of-body experiences, and more. We are advancing into expanded multidimensional awareness.

Angels are manifesting more dramatically, and in greater numbers, to help us in this transformation of consciousness.

### Finding the meaning in angel encounters

An encounter with an angel does not truly benefit us unless we are able to accept it as a real experience and integrate it into our worldview. Encounters with angels are part of a broader spectrum of unusual experiences that incorporate altered states of consciousness, nonordinary realities, psychic phenomena, and elements of the mystical. Various terms have been given these experiences, such as "extraordinary," "transcendent," "transpersonal," and "exceptional human experience." Psychologist Abraham H. Maslow, who pioneered humanistic and transpersonal psychologies, coined the term "peak experience" to describe nonreligious, quasi-mystical episodes as sudden flashes of intense happiness and well-being, and awareness of the "ultimate truth" and unity of all things. Such peak experiences can be part of angel experiences.

Because of the subjective and personal nature of such experiences, science is at a loss to deal with them. Religious approaches have their limits as well, having to remain within the confines of officially sanctioned teachings and dogma.

The ultimate evaluation depends on the individual experiencer. Angel encounters are transformative: a person is changed as a result of having one. For some, the change may be radical, and for others, it may be validation of a worldview already held. Every experiencer weighs an extraordinary encounter against personal, institutional and cultural beliefs.

Angels give us something positive and useful, whether it is information, inspiration, or reaffirmation of self-worth. They bring positive experiences that open up doorways to life, or doorways to other realities—or both. They connect us to the highest and deepest parts of ourselves, to each other, to all things, and to God.

Believing in angels, or thinking about angels, especially if one has had angel encounters, encourages more experiences of the same sort. Philosopher Michael Grosso calls this the "mirror factor of the psychic universe." The psychic universe reflects back to us what we believe, and we then experience what we believe. The stronger our beliefs, the more feedback we get in terms of experiences.

Everyone possesses the ability to make contact with angels, such as through visionary experience, clairaudience or the intuitive voice. "You have to want the communion, and make the commitment to the angels to work with them," said Jayne Howard Feldman. "Most of all, you have to be responsible. What are you going to do with the results? If you're sincere about growing and helping other people, the angels will be glad to work with you. Expect miracles."

One can invest too much in angels, however. As Ken Cohen observed, angels, totems, and other spiritual helpers should not be sought for themselves, but as aids to reach the Great Mystery.

The angels themselves had a similar message as channeled by Eddie Burks:

> Do not reduce us in any way to suit humanity's understanding. This would not be right. Raise humanity instead to meet us through inspired understanding. Impress on people that we are not as they. We are not human. We are no closer to God than you are. But we serve his purpose in a way that you would judge to be more direct.

Angels have often communicated to people that they cannot help unless they are asked. We can ask for help in many ways. Sometimes we ask for help unconsciously, that is, through our Higher Selves, or spontaneously in a moment of crisis. We can ask as part of our spiritual practice, through direct invitation, prayer, meditation, and visualization. While we can ask for ourselves, we will achieve far more if we ask for help for others—our angels working through the angels that protect other people, like some of the popes have done.

Always give thanks for the help, the blessings in life, and the opportunities that lie ahead. Give thanks for the guidance that is being sought. It will be given.

Remember the words of the angels:

*We bear the very essence of unconditional love.*

# About the Author

Rosemary Ellen Guiley is one of the leading experts in the metaphysical and paranormal fields. She is the author of more than 60 books, including several other books about angels and an authoritative *The Encyclopedia of Angels*. Her early angel experiences were a major influence in shaping the direction of her career as an author, researcher, and investigator. She has had angel experiences throughout life, and maintains her connection to the angelic realm through daily meditation and prayer.

Rosemary also works as a dreamwork facilitator for individuals and groups, and is a Dream Oracle dream interpreter on the DreamSocial. co website. She is a certified hypnotist and conducts regressions for past lives. She is a Tarot reader, and teaches the Tarot and psychic skills. In addition, she researches the afterlife, and investigates cases of paranormal activity and entity interferences and attachments.

Rosemary serves on the board of advisors for the Foundation for Research into Extraterrestrial Encounters, and is a former member of the board of directors of the International Association for the Study of Dreams. She lectures and teaches internationally on a wide range of subjects, is featured frequently in the media, including *Coast to Coast AM* with George Noory; and runs her own publishing company. She lives in Connecticut. Her website is www.visionaryliving.com.

# Bibliography and Suggested Reading

Burnham, Sophy. *A Book of Angels*. New York: Ballantine Books, 1990.

_____. *Angel Letters*. New York: Ballantine Books, 1991.

Cervelli, Roseann. *Voices of Love*. Farmingdale, NY: Coleman Publishing, 1986.

Daniel, Alma, Timothy Wyllie, and Andrew Ramer. *Ask Your Angels*. New York: Ballantine Books, 1992.

Davidson, Gustav. *A Dictionary of Angels*. New York: The Free Press, 1967.

Evans, Hilary. *Visions*Apparitions*Alien Visitors*. Wellingborough: Aquarian Press, 1984.

_____. *Gods*Spirits*Cosmic Guardians*. Wellingborough: Aquarian Press, 1987.

_____. *Alternate States of Consciousness*. Wellingborough, England: Aquarian Press, 1989.

Freeman, Eileen Eilas. *Touched by Angels*. New York: Warner Books, 1993.

Godwin, Malcolm. *Angels: An Endangered Species*. New York: Simon & Schuster, 1990.

Graham, Billy. *Angels: God's Secret Agents*. New York: Doubleday, 1975.

Grant, Jack. *Companions in Spirit*. Berkeley, CA: Celestial Arts, 1984.

Guiley, Rosemary Ellen. *The Encyclopedia of Angels*. 2nd ed. New York: Facts On File, 2004.

_____. *The Angels Tarot*. San Francisco: HarperSanFranciso, 1995.

_____. *Angels of Mercy*. New York: Pocket Books, 1994.

Hodson, Geoffrey. *The Brotherhood of Angels and Men*. Wheaton, IL: Quest Books, 1982. First published 1927.

Howard, Jane M. *Commune with the Angels*. Virginia Beach, VA: A.R.E. Press, 1992.

Huber, Georges. *My Angel Will Go Before You*. Westminster, MD: Four Courts Press, 1983.

Humann, Harvey. *The Many Faces of Angels*. Marina del Rey, CA: Devorss Publications, 1986.

Laurence, Richard (trans.). *The Book of Enoch the Prophet*. San Diego: Wizards Bookshelf, 1983.

Maclean, Dorothy. *To Hear the Angels Sing*. Hudson, NY: Lindisfarne Press, 1980.

MacGregor, Geddes. *Angels: Ministers of Grace*. New York: Paragon House 1988.

Mallasz, Gitta (transcribed). *Talking with Angels*. Einseideln: Daimon Verlag, 1988.

Moolenburgh, H.C. *A Handbook of Angels*. Walden, England: C.W. Daniel, 1984.

_____. *Meetings with Angels*. Walden, England: C.W. Daniel, 1991.

McLean, Adam (ed.). *A Treatise on Angel Magic*. Grand Rapids, MI: Phanes Press, 1990.

Parente, Fr. Allesio, O.F.M., Cap. *Send Me Your Guardian Angel*, Padre Pio. Foggia, Italy: Editions, 1961.

Parisen, Maria (comp.) *Angels & Mortals: Their Co-Creative Power*. Wheaton, IL: Quest Books, 1990.

Pseudo-Dionysius: *The Complete Works*. New York: Paulist Press, 1987.

Ronner, John. *Do You Have A Guardian Angel?* Murfreesboro, TN: Mamre Press, 1985.

Snell, Joy. *The Ministry of Angels*. New York: The Citadel Press, 1959.

Taylor, Terry Lynn. *Messengers of Light: The Angels' Guide to Spiritual Growth*. Tiburon, CA: HJ Kramer, 1990.

_____. *Guardians of Hope: The Angels' Guide to Personal Growth*. Tiburon, CA: HJ Kramer, 1992.

_____. *Answers from the Angels: A Book of Angel Letters*. Tiburon, CA: HJ Kramer, 1993.

Virtue, Doreen. *Angel Medicine*. Carlsbad, CA: Hay House: 2005.

Wyllie, Timothy. *Dolphins\*Extraterrestrials\*Angels*. Ft. Wayne, IN: Bozon Enterprises, 1984.

Made in the USA
Middletown, DE
18 April 2017